STUDENT STUD

Frank Schmalleger • Gordon Armstrong • William D. Head • Steven Chermak

CRIMINAL JUSTICE TODAY

FOURTH EDITION

Frank Schmalleger, Ph.D.

The Justice Research Association

PRENTICE HALL EDUCATION, CAREER, & TECHNOLOGY, UPPER SADDLE RIVER, NEW JERSEY 07458

Production Editor: *Janet M. McGillicuddy*
Acquisitions Editor: *Neil Marquardt*
Supplement Acquisitions Editor: *Judith Casillo*
Electronic Page Composition: *Janet M. McGillicuddy*
Director of Manufacturing and Production: *Bruce Johnson*
Manufacturing Buyer: *Ed O'Dougherty*

 ©1997 by Prentice-Hall, Inc.
A Simon & Schuster Company
Upper Saddle River, New Jersey 07458

Printed in the United States of America

10 9 8 7 6 5 4 3 2

ISBN 0-13-566365-2

Prentice-Hall International (UK) Limited, *London*
Prentice-Hall of Australia Pty. Limited, *Sydney*
Prentice-Hall Canada Inc., *Toronto*
Prentice-Hall Hispanoamericana, S.A., *Mexico*
Prentice-Hall of India Private Limited, *New Delhi*
Prentice-Hall of Japan, Inc., *Tokyo*
Simon & Schuster Asia Pte. Ltd., *Singapore*
Editora Prentice-Hall do Brasil, Ltda., *Rio de Janeiro*

CONTENTS

A LETTER FROM THE AUTHOR

Dear Criminal Justice Student:

I hope you will take a few minutes to read this letter since it may be my only chance, as the author of your textbook, *Criminal Justice Today*, to tell you how you can use my book and the student study guide which accompanies it to their fullest potential. I'd also like to tell you why I think it's important for you to be successful in your introductory course.

When I wrote *Criminal Justice Today* I hoped to be able to accomplish a number of things. Among them, I wanted to provide a textbook which would: 1.) teach beginning criminal justice students and others interested in the field, all the basic concepts and terminology they would need to intelligently analyze the process of American criminal justice as it unfolds on a daily basis on street corners, in courtrooms, and in correctional settings across the country; 2.) be the most current source available to prepare students to work within the criminal justice system of the twenty-first century; and 3.) provide a realistic conceptual framework that students could feel comfortable adopting, and which would help guide them in their thinking about the American criminal justice system of today, and of the future.

There is, however, a "higher purpose" in studying criminal justice—and it has to do with why you should want to be especially attentive to your instructor, to your textbook, to this study guide, and to the study of the subject matter which this course has to offer. Think of your course as a study in justice, and view your professor as a guide to justice issues in the modern world. Use your textbook, in combination with this study guide, other course materials, and the lectures your instructor provides, as a tool to evaluate the American criminal justice system relative to your own understandings of fairness and of right and wrong. If you do that, you will achieve the highest purpose I had in mind when I wrote *Criminal Justice Today*: you will be firmer in your understanding of the fact that "injustice anywhere is a threat to justice everywhere," and you will be a better citizen as a result.

To get the most out of *Criminal Justice Today*, I urge you to give serious attention to the theme of my book (which is discussed in the first chapter). Use the theme as a tool for analyzing the concepts and ideas you encounter in the chapters that follow. Pay special attention to the lofty ideal of social justice which is discussed in Chapter 1, and think seriously about what *justice* means to you in specific situations in everyday life. Ask yourself, as you read the textbook, whether justice is being done in the day-to-day practice of American criminal justice—and if it is not, how the criminal justice system can be improved.

If you have suggestions about improving *Criminal Justice Today*, if you have suggestions about any of our supplements, or if there are features you would like to see added to the next edition, I'd be happy to hear directly from you. Please write to me at: The Justice Research Association, P. O. Drawer 23557, Hilton Head Island, SC 29925, or e-mail me at: cjtoday@aol.com.

As you set out to study the American criminal justice system, my thoughts and best wishes for success go with you. Enjoy your course!

Sincerely,

Frank Schmalleger, Ph.D., Director
The Justice Research Association

*A*cknowledgments

A work as complex as the entire instructional package which comprises *Criminal Justice Today*, 4ed. requires the efforts of many dedicated and highly-skilled individuals. I am grateful to everyone who worked hard to insure quality in this manual. The initial materials for this publication were developed by Bill Head and Steve Chermak, and benefited considerably from the dedicated efforts of Gordon Armstrong. Janet McGillicuddy, who served as production editor for this volume worked ceaselessly to insure accuracy and quality, and Dave Moles electronically prepared this manual's contents for printing. The editorial assistance provided by Andrea Messer, Paul R. Odum II, and Shelia Cope Armstrong is also much appreciated. Coordinating all the supplements was the job of Prentice Hall supplements editor Judy Casillo. As she has done many times in the past on all of my Prentice Hall projects, Judy once again did an excellent job of pulling things together and insuring that deadlines were met. Thank you each and everyone!

Frank Schmalleger

INTRODUCTION

This study guide was created to be a supplemental learning tool to Frank Schmalleger's textbook, **Criminal Justice Today**. It is important that you read the chapters of the textbook carefully before using this study guide. We have designed the study guide to help you learn terms, cases, and ideas presented in the textbook's chapters. In addition, we have tried to put the materials discussed in the book into a broader perspective, allowing you to understand the application of Schmalleger's ideas to practical criminal justice situations. The chapters of this study guide correspond directly to the chapters of the textbook. Each study guide chapter is broken into five sections, as follows:

1. *Chapter Summary.* This section provides an overview of the general themes and ideas for each chapter.
2. *Learning Tips.* Tips included in the chapters are intended to help you learn the material in the text, but can also be applied to other courses and to your college career as a whole.
3. *Key Terms.* We have provided the terms that Professor Schmalleger has placed in the textbook margins to highlight their significance. We take those definitions verbatim and present them to you in one section so you have easy access to them. In addition, we provide examples to help you learn and understand the meaning of the terms.
4. *Practice Test Questions.* These were created to test your ability to comprehend the materials presented in the textbook. There are multiple choice, true/false, and a matching section in each chapter.
5. *Discussion Exercises.* These exercises were created to help you put the reading materials into a broader perspective, and generate discussion about important criminal justice issues. We have included newspaper articles in several chapters to assist you in responding to these questions.

If you have any questions or have suggestions on how this study guide can be made more helpful to you, please send your thoughts and comments to:

The Justice Research Association
Attn: Criminal Justice Today
P.O. Drawer 23557
Hilton Head Island, SC 29925

or e-mail: cjtoday@aol.com

Thank you

Steve Chermak, Ph.D.
Bill Head, Ph.D.
Gordon M. Armstrong, M.A.

WHAT IS CRIMINAL JUSTICE?

CHAPTER SUMMARY

In Chapter 1 the text meets three objectives. First, it provides a framework for struggling with difficult criminal justice issues. Second, it examines whether the criminal justice process functions as a system. Finally, it provides an overview of the book and of the criminal justice process.

Throughout the text you will be exposed to controversial criminal justice issues. For example, the author introduces you to "Megan's Law," a recently enacted New Jersey law which requires community notification whenever an imprisoned sex offender is scheduled to be released. How does the release of this information affect the defendant? Does it help the community? What are your reactions to the requirement that the public be notified when sex offenders are about to be released from confinement?

The author provides a framework to think about these difficult issues. This framework involves balancing individual rights (i.e., the right of individuals to be protected from overzealous and intrusive government agents) against community interests (i.e., the right of society to feel secure from crime. Individual rights and community interests are delicately balanced in our **criminal justice system**. When a movement is made to expand individual rights, such as in the 1960s, community interests are affected. Conversely, and more recently, as community interests have expanded, individual rights have been limited.

How one balances these two competing interests derives from each person's conception of justice. What is fair? Can the system be more fair? Everyone, including politicians, victims, defendants, police officers, prosecutors, and judges, attempts to balance individual and community interests, affecting how justice is conceptualized. Individuals who prefer to protect freedoms and liberties are called **individual rights advocates**. Individuals who believe that the interests of society should take precedence over liberties are called **public order advocates**. It is important to realize that 1) understandings of justice are different for everyone, and 2) our definitions are shaped by our life experiences.

The criminal justice system is the mechanism that has been established for meting out justice when criminal law violations occur. Yet, does the criminal justice system function as a system? Supporters of a **consensus model** of justice say "yes." This model argues that the system is predictable, that there is a high level of cooperation among agencies and individuals in the system, and that the components of the system—police, courts, and corrections—operate without conflict. Conversely, the **conflict model** of criminal justice views the operation of these components from a different perspective. Supporters of this model argue that the goals of criminal agencies and the individuals working within them differ, and that system processing is affected by outside influences such as political currents, informal arrangements, and discretion.

Both models have some value in understanding the operation of the criminal justice system. There are times when the agencies of criminal justice work closely together representing a consensus model. For example, when criminal justice crisis situations arise, such as when the federal building in Oklahoma City was bombed, each component was focused on similar goals. However, at other times, the goals of each agency conflict. A prosecutor may, for example, want police officers to crack down on juvenile crime. Police officers, however, may feel that other crimes, perhaps drunk driving, should take priority.

Finally, the author provides an overview of the book and introduces you to the stages in the justice process. It is important that you familiarize yourself with these stages. In general, the criminal justice process starts when a citizen (victim or witness) calls the police to report a crime. The police are responsible for conducting the **investigation**, making an **arrest** (if they can establish probable cause), and **booking** the suspect. The court process kicks in when this suspect appears before a judge at the **first appearance**. Here, the decision is made about what should be done with the suspect pending the outcome of the case. A **grand jury** or **preliminary hearing** will then be conducted to determine whether the criminal justice process should continue. An **information** results from a preliminary hearing, and an **indictment** results from a grand jury hearing, when this question is answered in the affirmative. The suspect then will be arraigned on the charges. A trial will be held, and if the person is found (or pleads) guilty, then **sentencing** occurs. It is then the responsibility of the corrections component of the criminal justice system to carry out the sentence.

LEARNING TIPS

THE SYLLABUS

The syllabus for a course is something that students tend to look at once or twice at the beginning of the semester and then disregard. Try to use the syllabus as a way of organizing your semester, preparing for each class, and gaining some insight into what the instructor considers important in the class. Many times, the instructor will include a brief overview of the course that could provide the key for essay or short answer/identification questions later in the semester.

PRE-CLASS REVIEW

One way to give yourself a head start is to arrive at class early. Review the notes from the preceding class meeting, and review sections that were assigned. This will help you recall the focus of the previous class, get your mind prepared for the present class, and may point out questions you intend to ask.

KEY TERMS

Social Control: The use of sanctions and rewards available through a group to influence and shape the behavior of individual members of that group. Social control is a primary concern of social groups and communities, and it is the interest that human groups hold in the exercise of social control that leads to the creation of both criminal and civil statutes.

Example: The behavior of prison inmates is influenced by both formal and informal rules. The informal rules are developed by inmates and are accepted over time as inmates become part of the prison subculture. Inmates violating these informal rules are punished. For example, one informal rule of prison life is "Don't snitch on other inmates." If an inmate violates this rule, he/she may be physically attacked by other inmates or killed.

Individual Rights Advocates: Those who seek to protect personal freedoms within the process of criminal justice.

Public Order Advocates: Those who suggest that, under certain circumstances involving criminal threats to public safety, the interests of society should take precedence over individual rights.

Individual Rights: Those rights guaranteed by the U.S. Constitution to criminal defendants facing formal processing by the criminal justice system. The preservation of the rights of criminal defendants is important to society because it is through the exercise of such rights that the values of our culture are most clearly and directly expressed.

> Example: The Fourth Amendment includes a provision guaranteeing protection against unreasonable search and seizures. "Thy Home is thy Castle," and if government agents want to gather evidence from our homes, persons, or effects that might be used as evidence at trial, they must obtain a search warrant based on probable cause or otherwise justify the search according to one of the numerous exceptions to the warrant requirement. (The Fourth Amendment is discussed in detail in Chapter 7, Policing: Legal Aspects.)

Justice: The principle of fairness; the ideal of moral equity.

Social Justice: An ideal that embraces all aspects of civilized life and is linked to fundamental notions of fairness and to cultural beliefs about right and wrong.

Criminal Justice: The criminal law, the law of criminal procedure, and that array of procedures and activities having to do with the enforcement of the criminal law. Criminal justice cannot be separated from social justice because the kind of justice enacted in our nation's criminal courts is a reflection of basic American understandings of right and wrong.

> Comment: This summarizes what the entire book is about. The criminal law is what is on the books; criminal procedures are the rules that must be followed by agents of justice when enforcing the law (i.e., reading *Miranda* rights prior to questioning, obtaining search warrants when required, etc.); and the procedures and activities are the array of decisions made by police, courts, and correctional officials in the processing of cases.

The Criminal Justice System: The aggregate of all operating and administrative or technical support agencies that perform criminal justice functions. The basic divisions of the operational aspects of criminal justice are law enforcement, courts, and corrections.

> Comment: In general, police agencies are responsible for investigating and arresting, courts are responsible for prosecuting and ensuring defendant's rights are not violated, and correctional agencies are responsible for punishing and rehabilitating.

Consensus Model: A perspective on the study of criminal justice that assumes that the system's subcomponents work together harmoniously to achieve that social product we call "justice."

> Comment: Illustrative of how the system is supposed to work, it assumes a high level of cooperation among the agencies.

Conflict Model: A perspective on the study of criminal justice which assumes that the system's subcomponents function primarily to serve their own interests. According to this theoretical framework, "justice" is more a product of conflicts among agencies within the system than it is the result of cooperation among component agencies.

> Comment: When goals conflict across agencies, dissension arises. Police departments might feel community pressure to respond to a gang problem, increasing the number

of arrests to give the appearance that something is being done. Prosecutors may, because of an overcrowded caseload, refuse to process these cases, resulting in charges being dropped.

Due Process of Law: A right guaranteed by the Fifth, Sixth, and Fourteenth Amendments of the U.S. Constitution, and generally understood, in legal contexts, to mean the due course of legal proceedings according to the rules and forms which have been established for the protection of private rights.

> Comment: (refer to "individual rights" definition above). Due process of law concerns the protections that have been put in place to provide individuals the tools essential to protect themselves against government.

Crime Control Model of Criminal Justice: A model, developed by Herbert Packer, to represent a decision-making process that favors the interests of the community over individual rights.

> Comment: A conservative criminal justice agenda is closely associated with the crime control model. This agenda includes protecting the community by increasing sentences for those suspects convicted of crime and limiting the rights of individuals.

Due Process Model of Criminal Justice: A model which represents the decision-making process that favors the need to protect individuals against injustices over community interests.

> Comment: A liberal criminal justice agenda is closely associated with the due process model. This agenda includes protecting the interests of individuals by providing them with additional rights and attempting to rehabilitate society to change individuals.

Probable Cause: A legal criterion residing in a set of facts and circumstances which would cause a reasonable person to believe that a particular person has committed a specific crime. Probable cause refers to the necessary level of belief which would allow for police seizures (arrests) of individuals and searches of dwellings, vehicles, and possession.

> Comment: Standard of proof needed for police officers to make an arrest and obtain a warrant to search for evidence.

Warrant: Any of a number of writs issued by a judicial officer which direct a law enforcement officer to perform a specified act and afford him protection from damage if he performs it.

Booking: A law enforcement or correctional administrative process of officially recording an entry into detention after arrest and identifying the person, the place, time, and reason for the arrest, and the arresting authority.

Bail: The money or property pledged to the court or actually deposited with the court to effect the release of a person from legal custody.

> Example: Cheryl Anderson is arrested and charged with two burglaries. At her first appearance, a judge who sets a $10,000 deposit bail. Ms. Anderson would be released if able to provide the court 10 percent ($1,000) of the bail. If released, she would be required to appear for all court proceedings.

Preliminary Hearing: The proceeding before a judicial officer in which three matters must be decided: whether a crime was committed, whether the crime occurred within the jurisdiction of the court, and whether there are reasonable grounds to believe that the defendant committed the crime.

Grand Jury: A body of persons who have been selected according to law and sworn to hear the evidence against accused persons and determine whether there is sufficient evidence to bring those persons to trial, to investigate criminal activity generally, and to investigate the conduct of public agencies and officials.

Indictment: A formal, written accusation submitted to the court by a grand jury, alleging that a specified person(s) has committed a specified offense(s), usually a felony. (contrast with information).

Information: A formal, written accusation submitted to a court by a prosecutor, alleging that a specified person(s) has committed a specified offense(s) (contrast with indictment).

Arraignment: The hearing before the court having jurisdiction in a criminal case, in which the identity of the defendant is established, the defendant is informed of the charges against and of his or her rights, and the defendant is required to enter a plea. (In some instances, any appearance in court prior to trial in criminal proceedings.)

Trial: The examination in a court of the issues of fact and law in a case, for the purpose of reaching a judgment of conviction or acquittal of the defendant(s).

> Comment: Typically, the trial phase of the court system will be shown in popular television dramas such as L.A. Law, Matlock, and Perry Mason. News coverage of celebrated cases, such as the O.J. Simpson case, also focuses on the trial phase of the criminal justice process.

Consecutive Sentence: A sentence that is one of two or more sentences imposed at the same time, after conviction, for more than one offense, and which is served in sequence with the other sentence(s); or a new sentence for new conviction added to a previous sentence.

> Example: Jody Riley was convicted of burglary and drug possession. She was sentenced to 3 years for the burglary and 3 years for the drug possession. If serving these sentences consecutively, she would first complete the sentence for the burglary, then serve the drug possession sentence (contrast with "concurrent sentence," below).

Concurrent Sentence: A sentence that is one of two or more sentences imposed at the same time, after conviction, for more than one offense and to be served at the same time, or a new sentence imposed upon a person already under sentence(s) for a previous offense(s), to be served at the same time as one or more of the previous sentences.

> Example: Jody Riley was convicted of burglary and drug possession. She was sentenced to 3 years for the burglary and 3 years for the drug possession. If serving these sentences concurrently, she would be serving both sentences at the same time (contrast with "consecutive sentence, above").

Criminology: The scientific study of crime causation, prevention, and the rehabilitation and punishment of offenders.

PRACTICE TEST QUESTIONS

MULTIPLE CHOICE

1-1. Which of the following models assumes a systems model of criminal justice?
    a. conflict model
    b. consensus model
    c. due process model
    d. individual rights model
    e. crime control model

1-2. What decision(s) is (are) made at a suspect's arraignment?
    a. The suspect is informed of the charges against him/her.
    b. The suspect is informed of his/her rights.
    c. The suspect is required to enter a plea.
    d. All of the above are decisions made at arraignment.

1-3. Who would support the full protection of personal freedoms and civil rights within the criminal justice process?
    a. an individual rights advocate
    b. a public order advocate
    c. a crime control advocate
    d. a justice ideal advocate

1-4. Who would suggest that under certain circumstances involving criminal threats to public safety the interests of society should take precedence over individual rights?
   a. an individual rights advocate
   b. a public order advocate
   c. a crime control advocate
   d. a justice ideal advocate

1-5. In the criminal justice process, a(n) _____ has to occur before _____.
   a. arrest; first appearance
   b. booking; arrest
   c. arraignment; preliminary hearing
   d. sentencing; trial
   e. all of the above

1-6. Who is credited with creating the crime control model of criminal justice?
   a. Colin Ferguson
   b. Herbert Packer
   c. Earl Warren
   d. Jerome Skolnick
   e. Bryan Freeman

1-7. The conflict model of criminal justice
   a. assumes that all parts of the system work together toward a common goal.
   b. assumes police officers are the dominant actors in the criminal justice system.
   c. assumes that the efforts of the component parts of the system are fragmented, leading to a criminal justice nonsystem.
   d. assumes that the movement of cases and people through the system is smooth due to cooperation between components of the system.
   e. all of the above

1-8. Upon being convicted of robbery and burglary, Jalen Arow is sentenced to 7 years for the robbery and 5 years for the burglary. The sentence for the burglary will be served in sequence to the robbery sentence. This is an example of
   a. a consecutive sentence.
   b. a concurrent sentence.
   c. an unfair sentence.
   d. a discriminatory sentence.

1-9. A(n) _____ is any of a number of writs issued by a judicial officer which direct a law enforcement officer to perform a specified act and afford him protection from damage if he performs it.
   a. pretrial release order
   b. information
   c. indictment
   d. warrant
   e. none of the above

1-10. A _____ is a body of persons sworn to hear the evidence against accused persons and determine whether, among other things, there is sufficient evidence to bring those persons to trial.
   a. grand jury
   b. preliminary hearing
   c. jury
   d. public forum

TRUE-FALSE

_____ 1-11. Expanding the rights of defendants to protect them from injustice would be most closely associated with a crime control model of criminal justice.

_____ 1-12. Criminal justice is more narrow than social justice in that it is concerned only with violations of criminal law.

_____ 1-13. A preliminary hearing is a body of persons selected according to law and sworn to hear the evidence against accused persons and determine whether there is sufficient evidence to bring those persons to trial.

_____ 1-14. Indictments are filed on the basis of the outcome of a preliminary hearing.

_____ 1-15. A concurrent sentence is when an offender, found guilty of more than one charge, is ordered to serve one sentence after another is completed.

_____ 1-16. The consensus model of the study of criminal justice assumes that the system's subcomponents function primarily to serve their own interests.

_____ 1-17. Bail is a mechanism that defendants use to avoid advancing into the latter stages of the criminal justice process.

_____ 1-18. Criminology is the application of scientific techniques to the investigation of a crime.

_____ 1-19. The *Miranda* decision only requires that police personnel advise a person of his/her rights at the time of the arrest.

_____ 1-20. Parole differs from probation in that offenders serve a portion of their prison sentences before being released.

MATCHING

a. Herbert Packer
b. public order advocate
c. individual rights advocate
d. social control
e. social justice
f. consensus model
g. conflict model
h. Jerome Skolnick
i. probable cause
j. beyond a reasonable doubt
k. booking
l. preliminary hearing
m. consecutive sentence
n. concurrent sentence

_____ 1-21. A perspective on the study of criminal justice which assumes that the system's subcomponents work together harmoniously to achieve that social product we call "justice."

_____ 1-22. His classic study of clearance rates provides support for the idea of a criminal justice nonsystem.

_____ 1-23. The person who first brought the crime control model to the attention of the academic community.

_____ 1-24. A legal criterion residing in a set of facts and circumstances which would cause a reasonable person to believe that a particular person has committed a specific crime.

_____ 1-25. Those who seek to protect personal freedoms within the process of criminal justice.

_____ 1-26. The step of the criminal justice process that occurs immediately after arrest.

_____ 1-27. An ideal which embraces all aspects of civilized life and which is linked to fundamental notions of fairness and to cultural beliefs about right and wrong.

_____ 1-28. The use of sanctions and rewards available through a group to influence and shape the behavior of individual members of that group.

_____ 1-29. A perspective on the study of criminal justice which assumes that the system's subcomponents function primarily to serve their own interests.

_____ 1-30. Those who suggest that, under certain circumstances involving criminal threats to public safety, the interests of society should take precedence over individual rights.

_____ 1-31. A sentence that is one of two or more sentences imposed at the same time after conviction for more than one offense, to be served at the same time

DISCUSSION EXERCISES

1. What is your definition of justice? (The discussion of justice in the text will be helpful for this exercise). Now consider the facts of the following case:

Dale and Mike Parak were twin brothers and best friends. They spent their entire lives looking out for each other's interests. When growing up, the two were inseparable. They played sports together, double dated frequently, and attended the same university. They grew closer as they aged, got married at about the same time, and eventually both were divorced. After they retired from their jobs, they decided to live together to save money and because they still enjoyed each other's company.

At the age of 70 years, Mike was diagnosed with cancer. Doctors predicted that he had about six months to live. The brothers, however, agreed that Mike should not suffer. Mike and Dale wrote and signed a note stating that they decided to commit suicide. Dale broke 20 tranquilizers into Mike's evening meal and watched as he ate it. Yet when Dale checked on Mike one hour later, Mike was still alive. Dale panicked. He took a .38 caliber revolver from his desk, and shot Mike, killing him instantly. He then went into the kitchen and took a handful of tranquilizers. He did not die. He awoke the next morning as somebody pounded on the front door. It was a neighbor who, when seeing that Dale was dazed and confused, decided to call an ambulance and the police.

The responding police officer conducted an investigation, and Dale was arrested and charged with the murder of his brother Mike. The prosecutor, although noting it to be a difficult case, pursued the case because she thought no citizen had the right to decide when someone should die. Dale Parak pled guilty to first-degree manslaughter and was sentenced to 5 years in a maximum security prison facility (note that this was the lowest sentence that could be given to a defendant convicted of this crime).

According to the definition of justice you provided, was this sentence just? Why or why not? If you were the prosecutor in this case, would you have charged Mr. Parak? Why or why not? If you were the judge in this case, how would you have sentenced Mr. Parak? Why? Compare your responses to your answers to the discussion questions asked in the textbook regarding the O.J. Simpson case.

2. Read the following *USA Today* story before answering the questions that follow.

Condemn Caning, Flogging: Torture Merits No Applause[1]

Singapore keeps ugly company, and Iran proves it. The same day American teenager Michael Fay was caned for vandalism in Singapore, officials in Tehran announced an American woman had been given 80 lashes for drunkenness.

The woman's confession — that "her job was corrupting young Iranians" — sounds coerced, which further strengthens the Iran-Singapore bond. Fay claims, with considerable supporting evidence, that his confession was forced, too.

Coerced confessions are not unusual in either nation, and predictably so. Legal systems that permit human beings to be flayed for drinking or vandalism usually have few compunctions about forcing the necessary statements of guilt first. The Inquisition operated in much the same way.

Yet, astoundingly, nearly half of all Americans think Singapore's canings show the way to improve security here.

They most emphatically do not.

True, Singapore's streets are famously clean and safe. But that's not just because the law allows experts in the martial arts to wound and scar those who behave in anti-social ways. They are clean and safe because Singaporeans tolerate a widespread loss of rights. Speech freedoms are restricted. Political independence is discouraged. Criminal suspects have no right to silence, no automatic right to trial.

Many nations have crime rates we would envy. But only 16 resort to canings or floggings. They include:

- Saudi Arabia, where a woman received 200 lashes for simply being accused of adultery;
- and the United Arab Emirates, where a 16-year-old got 550 lashes, meted out over three months, for drinking alcohol.

Lucky Michael Fay. Singapore reduced his punishment from six strokes to four in response to protests from Washington. But Fay's parents rightly point out that four scarring strokes is still torture. The milder sentence does nothing to mitigate Singapore's rejection of international conventions against torture.

When it comes to travel, you pay your money and take your chances. Local law is local law. But regardless of where it takes place, statutory corporal punishment — floggings or beatings or amputations and castrations — merits loud condemnation, not wishful applause.

You can pretend that justice with a stick is the same as a parent with a switch. But it's no coincidence that court-ordered corporal punishment is usually associated with truncated human and civil rights.

In Singapore, the streets are safe because some people are afraid to act out, and because everybody has been forced to compromise important rights and freedoms.

In the United States, Americans have every right to openly regret that surrender elsewhere in the world, and every obligation to fight a similar surrender here.

[1]*USA Today*, May 6, 1994, p. 10a.

You might remember the Fay case. Michael Fay was an 18-year-old American living with his parents in Singapore when arrested for spray-painting cars during 10 days of vandalism.[2] He confessed to these crimes, but later said that his confession was coerced from police officials who severely beat him. He was convicted and sentenced to four strokes with a rattan cane, a punishment where the prisoner is flogged, tearing open the skin and producing permanent scars. Based on your reading of the article above, and the facts of the case, answer the following questions.

Was the punishment imposed in this case a violation of Michael Fay's rights? Remember that his crime took place in Singapore, a legal system which balances individual and community rights very differently than our own. Indeed, over 1,000 prisoners are caned per year in Singapore. Do you think we should use similar types of punishment in the United States? How would corporal punishments, such as beating convicted violators with a rattan cane, affect individual rights? How would it impact community interests? How would an individual rights advocate respond? How would a public order advocate respond?

[2]"Overlooked Question in Singapore Caning Debate: Is the Teenager Guilty?" *The New York Times*, April 17, 1994.

C H A P T E R

THE CRIME PICTURE

CHAPTER SUMMARY

Mitchell Watts, while standing at a 10th Street bus stop, was approached by four teenagers who asked for his wallet. Although he said he didn't want any trouble and gave the teenagers his wallet without resistance, one of the teenagers hit Mitchell in the head with a baseball bat. He was knocked unconscious and was rushed to the hospital for his injuries.

How would these crimes be classified by the criminal justice system? The text describes various crime classification instruments in Chapter 2. For example, if Mitchell reported this incident to the police, it could eventually be part of that department's annual uniform crime statistics submitted to the FBI. If Mitchell's household was one of the households selected for the National Crime Victimization Survey, then his victimization could be included as part of these statistics. If the teenagers were arrested, a prosecutor might charge the youths with aggravated assault and robbery. If the facts from above were more detailed and included the additional information that Mr. Watts was an African American male and the teenagers spray painted a racial epithet on this back while unconscious, this crime might be classified as a hate crime.

The two primary sources of data used to understand the crime picture in America are official statistics and victimization statistics. The most cited and well-known official source of data are the **Uniform Crime Reports**, compiled annually by the FBI. There are approximately 20,000 police departments throughout the country which are asked to voluntarily submit statistics on crimes reported to them. The FBI compiles these statistics, then reports the figures as either **Part I offenses** or **Part II offenses**.

The best known source of victimization statistics is the **National Crime Victimization Survey**. This survey asks citizens directly about their victimization experiences, including characteristics of the perpetrator, the crime, and the incident. This survey includes information on six crimes: rape, robbery, assault, burglary, larceny, and motor vehicle theft.

Although both of these sources provide some general understanding of the crime problem, they are not without limitations. In developing the UCR, the FBI relies on the willingness of police departments to report all incidents and assumes that the information is accurately represented. But citizens, for a variety of reasons, may not want to involve the police. Fear of retaliation, embarrassment, or belief that the police cannot do anything about it anyway are cited as reasons for not reporting crimes. This reduces the accuracy of UCR data. Victimization statistics might present a more accurate portrait of crimes not reported to the police, but this source of data has other limitations. Respondents, for example, might lie or exaggerate the circumstances of their victimization.

The text also provides general descriptions of the eight **index offenses** and interesting descriptive information about each offense category. **Murder, forcible rape, aggravated assault, robbery, larceny, burglary, motor vehicle theft**, and **arson** are discussed in detail. **Murder**, for example, does not occur frequently (compared to the other index offenses), but when it does, the police are able to clear a large percentage of them (approximately 65%). When a murder does occur, young males (18–24 years old) are most likely to have committed this type of crime.

This chapter also has a section on women and crime, discussing women as both victims and offenders. Although women are not as likely as men to be victimized, they are more likely to be injured by crime and to be in fear of crime. Women are much less likely than males to commit one of the eight index offenses, although the rate that women commit these types of crime is increasing rapidly.

The text also introduces you to other ways of understanding the crime picture. It examines the criminal justice system's long-time interest in organized crime activities, and its more recent concern with hate crimes. It also discusses some of the economic costs of crime.

Although statistics are important to a general understanding of crime, their value is tempered by their inability to clearly indicate how crime affects individuals. Was Mr. Watts able to recover from his crimes physically? Psychologically? Emotionally? Was the criminal justice system responsive to his personal needs?

LEARNING TIPS

BINDERS

Three-ring binders are very advantageous. They allow for pages to be inserted or removed. Therefore, hand-outs, chapter notes, or notes from other classmates can be easily added, while unnecessary information can be removed. Additionally, during reviews, pages can be organized in a manner that allows the overall strategy of the lectures to be recognized more easily.

OFFICE HOURS

Very few students take advantage of posted office hours. As a consequence, very few students ever develop a relationship with the instructor, and most students are then hard-pressed to find a faculty member to write a recommendation letter, or help with career advice as their college years draw to a close. Most faculty members enjoy talking to students about the specific course or career opportunities in criminal justice. If you do go to an instructor's office hours, make sure you spend some time preparing in advance, creating a few questions on concepts from the class that might be unclear to you, or exploring some facet of the class that interests you.

KEY TERMS

Violent Crime: An offense category that, according to the FBI's Uniform Crime Reports, includes murder, rape, aggravated assault, and robbery.

> Comment: All of the crimes included in the violent crime category involve a direct confrontation between victim and defendant. The murders committed by Jeffrey Dahmer and the Milwaukee serial killer would all be considered violent crimes.

Property Crime: An offense category that, according to the FBI's *Uniform Crime Reports*, includes burglary, larceny, auto theft, and arson.

> Comment: Each of these crimes are generally less serious than the crimes in the violent crime offense category and usually do not include a face-to-face confrontation.

Crime Index: An inclusive measure of the violent and property crime categories of the UCR, also known as the "Part I offenses." The Crime Index has been a useful tool for geographic (state-to-state) and historical (year-to-year) comparative purposes because it employs the concept of a crime rate (the number of crimes per unit of population). However, the addition of arson as an eighth index offense in recent years, and the new executive branch requirements with regard to the gathering of "hate crime" statistics, have the potential to result in new crime index measurements which provide less than ideal comparisons.

> Comment: Includes the crimes of murder, rape, aggravated assault, robbery, burglary, larceny, auto theft, and arson. When reporting the Uniform Crime Reports statistics, the news media will typically present the figures for the crime index offenses.

Clearance Rate: A traditional measure of investigative effectiveness that compares the number of crimes reported and/or discovered to the number of crimes solved through arrest or other means (such as the death of a suspect).

> Example: If a police department received 10,000 reported incidents of rape in a year, and, of these 10,000 reported rapes were able to arrest 1,000 suspects, the clearance rate for rape in that city would be 10 percent.

Hierarchy Rule: In the *Uniform Crime Reports*, the hierarchy rule is used when counting the number of crimes in that jurisdiction. Only the most serious crime out of a series of events is scored.

> Example: If a victim reported an aggravated assault, larceny, and arson to the police, only the aggravated assault would be reported to the FBI.

Murder: The unlawful killing of a human being. Murder is a generic term, which in common usage may include first and second degree murder as well as "manslaughter," "involuntary manslaughter," and other, similar kinds of offenses.

> Example: Barney Armstrong was beaten over the head with a golf club by Fred Jones. When Mr. Armstrong died from his injuries, Jones was charged with his murder.

Forcible Rape: Unlawful sexual intercourse with a female, by force and against her will, or without legal or factual consent. Statutory rape differs from forcible rape in that it involves sexual intercourse with a female who is under the age of consent—regardless of whether or not she is a willing partner.

> Example: When Jim Thompson struck Mandy Starr, dragged her into an alley, and forced sexual intercourse with her, he committed forcible rape.

Date Rape: Unlawful, forced sexual intercourse with a female against her will which occurs within the context of a dating relationship.

> Comment: High-profile cases, such as the arrests of William Kennedy Smith and Mike Tyson, have created much interest in rapes that occur when the parties have a prior relationship.

Robbery: The unlawful taking or attempted taking of property that is in the immediate possession of another, by force or the threat of force. Armed robbery differs from unarmed or strong-armed robbery with regard to the presence of a weapon. Contrary to popular conceptions, highway robbery does not necessarily occur on a street — and rarely in a vehicle. Highway robbery is a term applicable to any form of robbery which occurs in a public place and out of doors.

> Example: Carl Rankin was charged with robbery after holding up a store with a cup of hot coffee. Mr. Rankin robbed the cashier after dousing her with coffee.

Assault: The unlawful intentional inflicting, or attempted or threatened inflicting, of injury upon the person of another. Historically, "assault" meant only the attempt to inflict injury on another person. A completed act constituted the separate offense of battery. Under most modern penal codes, however, attempted and completed acts are put together under the generic name "assault." While the names "aggravated assault" and "simple assault" are standard terms for reporting purposes, most state penal codes use labels such as "first degree," "second degree," etc. to make such distinctions.

> Example: On his way home from work, Kyle Neil was surrounded by four teenage girls. Natalie Jones punched Kyle in the face, committing an assault.

Burglary: The unlawful entry of any fixed structure, vehicle, or vessel used for regular residence, industry, or business, with or without force, with intent to commit a felony or larceny. For UCR purposes, the crime of burglary can be reported if: 1) an unlawful entry of an unlocked structure has occurred, 2) a breaking and entering (of a secured structure) has taken place, or 3) a burglary has been attempted.

> Example: A woman, who used a ladder to enter a second-story apartment window committed burglary when she stole the owner's pet boa constrictor named Bill.

Larceny: The unlawful taking or attempted taking of property other than a motor vehicle from the possession of another, by stealth, without force and without deceit, with intent to permanently deprive the owner of the property. Larceny is the most common of the eight major offenses—although probably only a small percentage of all larcenies which occur are actually reported to the police because of the small dollar amounts involved.

> Example: Jason Arnold committed larceny when he walked out of a grocery story without paying for a six-pack of beer.

Motor Vehicle Theft: The unlawful taking or attempted taking of a self-propelled road vehicle owned by another, with the intent to deprive him or her of it permanently or temporarily. The stealing of trains, planes, boats, construction equipment, and most farm machinery is classified as larceny under the UCR reporting program—not as motor vehicle theft.

> Example: A type of motor vehicle theft that has gotten publicity recently is 'carjacking'. Typically, after the victim unlocks the door, the carjacker will threaten the owner with a weapon and steal the car with or without the victim in it.

Arson: The unlawful, willful, or malicious burning or attempted burning of property with or without intent to defraud. Some instances of arson are the result of malicious mischief, while others involve attempts to claim insurance money. Still others are committed in an effort to disguise other crimes, such as murder, burglary, and larceny.

> Example: You might be familiar with drug-sniffing dogs. However, you might not know that dogs are also trained to sniff out arson. These dogs are used to detect fuels, such as gasoline, which are commonly used to commit arson.

Hate Crimes: Criminal offenses in which there is evidence of prejudice based on race, religion, sexual orientation, or ethnicity.

> Example: When four skinheads broke windows and spray painted graffiti on a Jewish community center, hate crimes were committed.

Organized Crime: The unlawful activities of the members of a highly organized, disciplined association engaged in supplying illegal goods and services, including but not limited to gambling, prostitution, loansharking, narcotics, labor racketeering, and other unlawful activities of members of such organizations.

PRACTICE TEST QUESTIONS

MULTIPLE CHOICE

2-1. Which of the following offense categories include crimes such as larceny and arson?
a. violent crime
b. property crime
c. hate crime
d. organized crime

2-2. Which of the following is not one of the *Uniform Crime Reports* Part I offenses?
a. murder
b. rape
c. drug possession
d. motor vehicle theft
e. burglary

2-3. Which of the following is not a problem with *Uniform Crime Reports* statistics?
a. Certain crimes are rarely reported to the police.
b. Only the most serious crime, when a number of crimes are committed, will be included in these reports.
c. Victims may believe that the police cannot do anything about a crime, so they do not report it to them.
d. No real attempt has been made to create divisions with nearly equal populations or similar demographic characteristics, and it is difficult to meaningfully compare one region of the country with another.
e. All of the above are problems.

2-4. Which of the following agencies is responsible for compiling the *Uniform Crime Reports*?
a. Bureau of Justice Statistics
b. Federal Bureau of Investigation
c. United States Marshals Service
d. Office of Juvenile Justice and Delinquency

2-5. Which Part I offense is most likely to be reported to the police?
a. larceny
b. rape
c. robbery
d. motor vehicle theft
e. aggravated assault

2-6. What is the most cited reason why rape victims do not report the crime to the police?
a. fear of embarrassment
b. police cannot do anything about it
c. not worth the victim's time
d. fear of reprisal

2-7. The National Crime Victimization Survey does not include information about which crime?
a. household larceny
b. motor vehicle theft
c. robbery
d. murder
e. burglary

2-8. Megan Anderson unlawfully entered a computer services building and stole a laser printer. What crime did she commit?

     a. robbery
     b. burglary
     c. aggravated assault
     d. forcible rape

2-9. The stealing of a train would be classified under what category of the UCR?
     a. larceny
     b. motor vehicle theft
     c. burglary
     d. robbery
     e. all of the above

2-10. Which of the following is not a victimless crime?
     a. drug use
     b. prostitution
     c. gambling
     d. motor vehicle theft
     e. all of the above

TRUE–FALSE

_____ 2-11. Violent crimes are generally more serious than property offenses.

_____ 2-12. *Uniform Crime Reports* statistics contain detailed descriptions of the personal lives of crime victims.

_____ 2-13. White-collar crimes, such as embezzlement, fraud, and insider trading, are all Part I offenses.

_____ 2-14. Clearance rates refer to the proportion of crimes that are reported to the police.

_____ 2-15. All women secretly desire to be raped.

_____ 2-16. Robbery is a crime against property; burglary is a personal crime.

_____ 2-17. The *Uniform Crime Reports* employ a hierarchical counting system, counting only the most serious incidents in a series of events.

_____ 2-18. Individuals most likely to be victimized by crime are also most likely to fear crime.

_____ 2-19. Although women are far less frequently victimized by crime compared to men, they are more likely to be injured by crime.

_____ 2-20. The UCR categories are legal classifications gleaned from the federal criminal code.

MATCHING

     a. aggravated assault   f. motor vehicle theft
     b. simple assault   g. forcible rape
     c. hate crimes   h. statutory rape
     d. organized crime   i. date rape
     e. larceny   j. gambling

_____ 2-21. The least reported of all violent index crimes.

_____ 2-22. A type of assault that includes the use of a weapon or the need for medical assistance for the victim.

_____ 2-23. Criminal offenses in which there is evidence of prejudice based on race, religion, sexual orientation, or ethnicity.

_____ 2-24. The most common of the eight major index offenses.

_____ 2-25. The index offense that is most likely to be reported to the police.

_____ 2-26. A type of assault involving pushing or shoving.

_____ 2-27. The unlawful activities of the members of a highly organized, disciplined association engaged in supplying illegal goods and services.

_____ 2-28. Unlawful, forced sexual intercourse with a female against her will which occurs within the context of a dating relationship.

_____ 2-29. Criminal offense considered by some to be a victimless crime.

_____ 2-30. Offense that involves sexual intercourse with a female who is under the age of consent — regardless of whether or not she is a willing partner.

DISCUSSION EXERCISES

1. An increasing number of campus police departments are reporting the offenses reported to them to the FBI's Uniform Crime Reporting Division. See if you can obtain the official crime statistics for your college. The discussion on the UCR in Chapter 2 indicates that this data source has limitations. One way to discover a more accurate picture of campus crime is to supplement UCR data with victimization statistics. Design a twenty-question victimization survey that could be used to supplement official statistics. What questions would you include? Why? What types of crimes would you ask about? Why? Compare the victimization statistics you gathered to the campus crime statistics found in the UCR for your college. (Be sure to read the discussion of the UCR and NCVS in Chapter 2 before completing this assignment.)

2. A prominent politician indicates that he would like to add a number of gang provisions to an anti-crime bill. He wants more information before firmly proposing what this legislation would look like. First, he needs to know whether gang-related crime incidents are a significant problem in America. If this politician asked you, what would you recommend as the best source of data to use to establish whether gang-related crimes are a problem? Why? What are the weaknesses of using the data source you recommend?

3. Go to the library and find the most recent publication of the *Uniform Crime Reports*. Record the results presented for the Part I offenses in your hometown and the town where your campus is located. Are the numbers different? If yes, why do you think the numbers are different? If no, why do you think the numbers are the same? Do you consider your hometown to be safe? Is your campus safe?

3

THE SEARCH FOR CAUSES

CHAPTER SUMMARY

Chapter 3 provides an overview of theories used to explain the causes of crime. The chapter begins with a discussion of the recent interest in "gangsta rap" and heavy metal music as possible causes of crime. It then discusses what a theory is and highlights the steps in the theory building process.

Chapter 3 focuses on various theories used to explain criminal behavior. Table 3-1 is an extraordinarily useful tool for its summary of the different characteristics of these theories and who is most noted for their development.

The first criminological theories discussed in Chapter 3 are from the **Classical School**, including the works of **Cesare Beccaria** and **Jeremy Bentham**. The text discusses the five basic assumptions of classical theory, which are summarized below:

1. Crime is caused by the individual exercise of free will.
2. Pain and pleasure are the two central determinants of human behavior.
3. Crime disparages the quality of bond which exists between individuals and society.
4. Punishment is necessary to deter law violators and serve as an example to others.
5. Crime prevention is possible through swift and certain punishment.

Theories in the **Biological School** search for causal explanations of crime in the body. Influenced by medical and technological advances, these theories have evolved over time. Compare the early biological theories of **Gall**, **Lombroso**, and **Sheldon** to contemporary biochemical theories. **Gall** argued that skull shape determined personality and behavior. **Lombroso** considered various parts of the body in his **atavistic** explanation for crime. Criminals, he argued, were throwbacks to earlier stages of evolution. **William Sheldon** used **somatotyping** (or body typing) to categorize each individual's physique by its **mesomorphic**, **endomorphic**, and **ectomorphic** characteristics. Sheldon found that juveniles with dominant mesomorphic physiques were most likely to commit crime. Biological inheritance as applied to criminal families has been considered in **Richard Dugdale's** examination of the Jukes' family tree and **Henry Goddard's** study of the Kallikaks.

Biological theories have advanced with medical technology. For example, chromosome theories look to internal gene structure to understand the causes of crime. The **XYY chromosome theory** was popular in the 1960s and early 1970s, but later studies question the ability of XYY theory to predict criminal behavior. Other biological theories have examined the effects of chemical imbalances, hormones, and allergic reactions to food on criminal behavior.

Psychological explanations argue that criminal behavior results from inappropriately conditioned behavior or from abnormal, dysfunctional, or inappropriate mental processes within the personality. One thread of psychological theories presented in the text is **behavioral conditioning**. Another thread focuses on personality disturbances and diseases of the mind. Conditioning holds that the frequency of any behavior can be increased through rewards, punishments, and/or association with other stimuli. **Sigmund Freud** argued that personality was developed from the interaction of the id, the ego, and the superego. One source of criminal behavior is the inability of a person's superego to control his/her id.

Sociological explanations of crime examine how such environmental forces as poverty, urban decay, and unemployment affect behavior. For example, **Shaw and McKay's social ecology theory** argues that certain areas of a city—those with high rates of poverty, unemployment, and a lack of schooling—are socially disorganized and likely to produce crime. **Anomie** is another sociological theory of crime. This theory concerns itself with the goals of society and the means to achieve goals. **Merton**, borrowing the concept of anomie from **Emile Durkheim**, argued that since the means to achieve goals are not equally available to all groups, individuals are forced to use illegitimate means, such as crime, to accomplish goals. On the other hand, **subcultural theories** argue that the goals of various groups are different and some groups view committing crime as a legitimate goal. For example, **Marvin Wolfgang** and **Franco Ferracuti** found that murder was an acceptable goal for certain groups.

Chapter 3 also discusses **social-psychological theories, conflict theories, phenomenological theories**, and some emerging theories, such as **feminist criminology**. Social-psychological theories explain deviant behavior by relating it to the cultural environment in which the individual matures. **Conflict theories** consider law to be a tool of the powerful, and is used to further their own interests. The **phenomenological school** argues that crime results from an active process of interpretation and social definition.

None of these theories provide a definitive explanation of why people commit crime. However, understanding how these theories explain the causes of crime is important because of the impact they have on the development of criminal justice policy and how the criminal justice system responds to crime.

LEARNING TIPS

WHEN TO STUDY

While students tend to study favorite subjects first, difficult and boring subjects require more energy and creativity. Thus, subjects which are difficult or boring need to be addressed early, saving more enjoyable coursework for later. However, if you find yourself continually avoiding a subject, this might indicate a serious trouble area. Therefore, you may need to seek help from a professor or tutorial service.

WHERE TO STUDY

Find a place where you will be alert, such as the library where there is good lighting and a low noise level. Once a place is found, regularly use this place to study until your mind and body are trained to recognize the area as your study place. Utilize this area exclusively for studying. Avoid watching television, eating, and socializing in your study place. Therefore, whenever you arrive at your study place, you will be able to focus your attention immediately.

KEY TERMS

Crime: Behavior in violation of the criminal laws of a state, the federal government, or a local jurisdiction which has the power to make such laws.

Deviance: A violation of social norms defining appropriate or proper behavior under a particular set of circumstances. Deviance often includes acts which are criminal.

> Example: A man who dresses like a woman, although not committing a crime, is generally considered to be displaying deviant behavior.

Theory: A series of interrelated propositions that attempt to describe, explain, predict, and ultimately control some class of events. A theory gains explanatory power for inherent logical consistency and is "tested" by how well it describes and predicts reality.

Research: The use of standardized, systematic procedures in the search for knowledge.

Hypothesis: 1. An explanation that accounts for a set of facts and that can be tested by further investigation... 2. [s]omething that is taken to be true for the purpose of argument or investigation.

> Example: If a scholar was examining what types of crime are presented in the news media, her hypothesis might be that murders are the type of crime most likely to be presented in the news. She would then conduct a research study to test this hypothesis.

Classical School: An eighteenth-century approach to crime causation and criminal responsibility which resulted from the Enlightenment and which emphasized the role of free will and reasonable punishments.

Biological School: A perspective on criminological thought which holds that criminal behavior has a physiological basis. Genes, foods and food additives, hormones, and inheritance are all thought to play a role in determining individual behavior. Biological thinkers highlight the underlying animalistic aspect of being human as a major determinate of behavior.

Atavism: A condition characterized by the existence of features thought to be common in earlier stages of human evolution.

> Comment: Cesare Lombroso thought criminals were atavists. He argued that certain physical characteristics, such as having huge jaws and canine teeth, predicted an individual's criminality.

Psychological School: A perspective on criminological thought which views offensive and deviant behavior as the products of dysfunctional personalities. The conscious, and especially the subconscious, contents of the human psyche are identified by psychological thinkers as major determinants of behavior.

Dangerousness: The likelihood that a given individual will later harm society or others. Dangerousness is often measured in terms of recidivism, or as the likelihood of additional crime commission within a five-year period following arrest or release from confinement.

Behavioral Conditioning: A psychological principle which holds that the frequency of any behavior can be increased or decreased through reward, punishment, and/or association with other stimuli.

Psychoanalysis: A theory of human behavior, based upon the writings of Sigmund Freud, which sees personality as a complex composite of interacting mental entities.

Psychopath (also sociopath): A person with a personality disorder, especially one manifested in aggressively antisocial behavior, which is often said to be the result of a poorly developed superego.

Psychosis: A form of mental illness in which sufferers are said to be out of touch with reality.

Schizophrenics: Mentally ill individuals who suffer from disjointed thinking and, possibly, delusions and hallucinations.

Anomie: A socially pervasive condition of normlessness. A disjuncture between approved goals and means.

Subculture of Violence: A cultural setting in which violence is a traditional method of dispute resolution.

> Example: A "beatdown," part of a gang initiation ceremony, involves a fight between a new member of a gang and the entire remaining members of the gang for a full minute. If the new member survives the violent attack, they become a respected member of the gang.

Social-Psychological School: A perspective on criminological thought which highlights the role played in crime causation by weakened self-esteem and meaningless social roles. Social-psychological thinkers stress the relationship of the individual to the social group as the underlying cause of behavior.

Moral Enterprise: The process undertaken by an advocacy group in order to have its values legitimated and embodied in law.

> Example: Mothers Against Drunk Driving (MADD) has been a very effective advocacy group since its inception in the mid-1970s. MADD has taken an active role in changing legislation on drunk driving.

Radical Criminology: A conflict perspective which sees crime as engendered by the unequal distribution of wealth, power, and other resources, which it believes is especially characteristic of capitalist societies. Also called "critical" and "Marxist" criminology.

Conflict Perspective: A theoretical approach which holds that crime is the natural consequence of economic and other social inequities. Conflict theorists highlight the stresses which arise between and within social groups as they compete with one another for resources and survival. The social forces which result are viewed as major determinants of group and individual behavior, including crime.

Phenomenological Criminology: A perspective on crime causation which holds that the significance of criminal behavior is ultimately knowable only to those who participate in it. Central to this school of thought is the belief that social actors endow their behavior with meaning and purpose. Hence, a crime might mean one thing to the person who commits it, quite another to the victim, and something far different still to professional participants in the justice system.

Feminist Criminology: A developing intellectual approach which emphasizes gender issues in the subject matter of criminology.

Peacemaking Criminology: A perspective which holds that crime control agencies and the citizens they serve should work together to alleviate social problems and human suffering and thus reduce crime.

PRACTICE TEST QUESTIONS

MULTIPLE CHOICE

3-1. Which school explains criminal behavior by looking at gene structure, hormones, and inheritance?

  a. Biological school
  b. Psychological school
  c. Sociological school
  d. Social-Psychological school
  e. Classical school

3-2. Which school emphasizes the role of free will and reasonable punishments?
  a. Biological school
  b. Psychological school
  c. Sociological school
  d. Social-Psychological school
  e. Classical school

3-3. Each of the following theorists are biological criminologists except _____.
  a. Franz Gall
  b. Jeremy Bentham
  c. Cesare Lombroso
  d. William Sheldon

3-4. Atavism is
  a. a term used to describe males with an extra Y chromosome.
  b. a term used to describe ectomorphic body types.
  c. a condition characterized by an individual with a dysfunctional superego.
  d. a condition characterized by the existence of features thought to be common in earlier stages of human evolution.

3-5. Which of the following sociological theories argues that crime is most likely to occur in "zones of transition?"
  a. anomie
  b. social ecology
  c. subcultural
  d. profiling

3-6. Which of Sheldon's body types has a relative predominance of muscle, bone, and connective tissue?
  a. endomorphs
  b. ectomorphs
  c. mesomorphs
  d. risomorphs

3-7. According to Robert Merton, a(n) _____ accepts both the goals of society and the means to achieve society's goals.
  a. conformist
  b. innovator
  c. retreatist
  d. ritualist
  e. rebel

3-8. _____ theory proposes that when an individual's bond to society weakens, the likelihood of crime increases.
  a. Containment
  b. Social control
  c. Labeling
  d. Differential association

3-9. Who would be considered a contemporary, or modern-day, biological theorist?
  a. Sarnoff Mednick
  b. James Q. Wilson
  c. Richard Herrnstein
  d. Both A and B
  e. all of the above

3-10. Each of the following theories can be considered social-psychological theories except:
   a. differential association.
   b. containment.
   c. social control.
   d. restrain.
   e. social ecology.

TRUE–FALSE

_____ 3-11. Cesare Lombroso is considered the founder of the Classical School of criminology.

_____ 3-12. The Biological School adopts as one of its basic assumptions that offensive and deviant behavior is the product of environmental forces.

_____ 3-13. Phrenologists study the shape of the skull to predict criminal behavior.

_____ 3-14. Anomie exists when there is a disjuncture between the goals of society and the means to achieve those goals.

_____ 3-15. Differential association theory was developed by Edwin Sutherland.

_____ 3-16. Techniques of neutralization are rationalizations which allow offenders to shed feelings of guilt for their behavior.

_____ 3-17. Cesare Beccaria is considered the "father of criminology."

_____ 3-18. Robert Merton's ritualist accepts both the goals and means which society consider legitimate.

_____ 3-19. Peacemaking criminology is considered a type of biological theory of crime.

_____ 3-20. Ectomorphs have bodies which are characterized by thinness, fragility, and delicacy.

MATCHING

   a. Jeremy Bentham
   b. Sigmund Freud
   c. Cesare Lombroso
   d. Travis Hirschi
   e. Franz Gall
   f. William Sheldon
   g. Cesare Beccaria
   h. Freda Adler
   i. Howard Becker
   j. Edwin Sutherland
   k. Marvin Wolfgang
   l. Robert Merton
   m. Hal Pepinsky
   n. Henry McKay

_____ 3-21. This was the person who worked with Clifford Shaw to develop social ecology theory.

_____ 3-22. The theorist who developed differential association theory.

_____ 3-23. The theorist who applied anomie to criminology.

_____ 3-24. The theorist who wrote the book *Sisters in Crime*.

_____ 3-25. He is referred to as the "father of modern criminology."

_____ 3-26. The founder of the Classical School of criminology.

_____ 3-27. This person is a subcultural theorist.

_____ 3-28. The name most widely associated with the field of psychology.

_____ 3-29. This theorist argues that crime results from social definition, through law, unacceptable behavior.

____ 3-30. One theorist who has popularized peacemaking criminology.

____ 3-31. The theorist who focused on the head and brain, calling his approach "cranioscopy."

____ 3-32. This theorist devised hedonistic calculus.

____ 3-33. The theorist who developed social control theory.

____ 3-34. This theorist used somatotyping to explain juvenile criminal behavior.

DISCUSSION EXERCISES

1. In Chapter 2, the author introduced you to the term "serial killer," described as someone who kills several victims in three or more separate events. In part because of the movie *Silence of the Lambs*, serial murder has received incredible amounts of news coverage. Serial murderers discussed in your book include Ted Bundy, John Gacy, and Jeffrey Dahmer. Read the article below that appeared in *USA Today*.

   Use the previous article and the materials in Chapter 3 to develop a theory on serial killing. Who becomes a serial killer? Why? Develop a criminological theory to explain serial murder. You can borrow from the theories described in Chapter 3, but try to create your own theory to explain this phenomenon. Figure 3-1 on how to build a theory is an excellent place to start. How would you test your theory? How does understanding Dahmer's background help in developing your theory?

A 13-Year Tale of Horror
Investigators Trace Dahmer's Gruesome Trail
As a Teen, Behavior was "On the Edge"[1]

Gawkers circled and neighbor kids sold lemonade Tuesday while police dug up the yard of Jeffrey Dahmer's boyhood home in Bath, Ohio.

They found evidence of what Dahmer said he buried there 13 years ago. Police believe more than 50 shards of bone they found are from the first man he killed.

Miles away, Milwaukee still recoils from Dahmer's later, calculated killings.

Dahmer has confessed to 17 killings in a serial of seduction, mutilation and cannibalism that started when he was 18. Formally charged with four murders, the 31-year-old former chocolate-factory worker has all but built the case against himself, even pointing

police to the spot where he buried his first victim.

Milwaukeeans blame their police force—and each other—for ignoring clues that might have unmasked Dahmer sooner. Some say bigoted disregard for those Dahmer killed—primarily gay and black men—led the community to ignore that something was terribly wrong in Dahmer's seedy apartment.

More precisely, say criminologists, something is terribly wrong in Dahmer—and probably has been for years. They contend that long before he killed, he carried the psychological seeds of his cruel acts.

High-school friends from Richfield, Ohio, recall a heavy-drinking prankster, so odd sometimes that

classmates avoided him. "He was tortured and lost at a very early age," says Mart Schmidt, a high-school friend. "I feel sorry for that."

He was given to stunts that were a step over the line. Classmates eventually came to categorize any bout of foolishness as "doing a Dahmer."

But some of his friends were drawn to his antics. "His behavior was always on the edge," says Schmidt. "Sometimes that was fun."

Schmidt, a sociology professor specializing in sexual abuse, recalls a class trip to Washington, D.C. As students discussed how to spend free time, Dahmer walked to a pay phone and brazenly arranged a tour of Vice President Mondale's office.

As the group walked to the White House, Dahmer feigned a seizure. "He fell on top of me," say Schmidt. "I said, 'How could you do that?' He said, 'I like to shake people up.'"

Dahmer killed for the first time a month before his parents' divorce was final, while he was alone in the family home. The breakup "was traumatic for him," says ex-classmate Cynthia Cassel.

Robert Ressler, a longtime FBI criminal investigator who has studied the nation's most notorious sexual serial killers, says such individuals usually come from troubled homes.

By adolescence, he says, they are "introverted and weird" youths who may contain their fantasies of sexual violence—or act them out.

Days after his high-school graduation, Dahmer picked up 19-year-old hitchhiker Steven Hicks, took him home for beers, then clubbed him with a barbell and strangled him.

Dahmer dismembered the body and buried it in his parents' yard.

Three months later, he started at Ohio State University. He left after just one term, joined the Army in 1979, and was booted out after two years for alcohol abuse.

Dahmer lived with his grandmother in a Milwaukee suburb for six years in the mid-1980s —when, he told police, he killed three men.

Police believe he took the acid-washed skull of one with him when he moved downtown.

Though psychologist Ressler says practice makes serial sexual killers better at hiding their crimes, the community ignored some signs of Dahmer's ghastly routine:

■ Neighbors who heard a young child's cries from Dahmer's apartment never called police.

Nor did the neighbors who heard a power saw buzzing at all hours.

■ Everyone in the 30-unit building where Dahmer lived noticed the smell of rotting flesh but accepted Dahmer's explanation that his freezer broke and some meat had spoiled.

■ Dahmer's probation officer did not visit his home, getting a requirement waived because of a heavy caseload and the rough neighborhood in which Dahmer lived.

■ Dahmer may have phoned victims' families. The Milwaukee Sentinel reported Tuesday that each of four families got an ominous call shortly after a relative disappeared.

"He just said, 'Don't bother looking for your brother,'" says Caroline Smith, whose brother Eddie was among the victims. "I said, "Why not?" He said, 'Because he's dead.' I said, 'How do you know that?' And he said, 'Because I killed him.'"

"A chill went through me."

She called police.

Perhaps most stunning, police visited Dahmer in May but came away blind to the horrors he wrought.

Police responded to a report of a naked, bleeding 14-year-old boy staggering outside Dahmer's building. But Dahmer convinced officers the boy was his adult homosexual partner and that they had a spat.

The officers left. Had they checked his record, they would have found that Dahmer was paroled 13 months earlier on a sexual-assault conviction. They also might have learned the boy was the younger brother of the boy Dahmer was convicted of molesting.

And they might have found the mutilated bodies of seven young men—four fewer victims than the 11 found when Dahmer was arrested.

Black and gay leaders say Dahmer was allowed to prey on their communities because the police hold them in such low esteem.

"Not only were these men the victims of a mass murderer but also of a police department that did not even notice, much less act upon, the disappearances of so many young men, most of whom were gay and African American," says Scott Gunkel of Lambda Rights Network, a gay-rights group.

The three officers who encountered Dahmer in May have been suspended with pay. The Milwaukee Police Association, calling the suspensions unfair, is asking 1,600 members for a no-confidence vote on Police Chief Phillip Arreola.

Arreola ordered an internal investigation expected to be completed in the next few days. The no-confidence vote is expected Friday.

Since his March 1990 parole on the sexual-assault charge, Dahmer has killed at least ten men.

One of them was Tony Hughes. At a packed memorial service for him Tuesday, there was a call for unity.

"Send your spirit into our communities," prayed Pastor E. Allen Sorum. "Bring us together in strength and hope and joy."

[1]Debbie Howlett and Patricia Edmonds, *USA Today*, July 31, 1991, p. 1a.

2. Chapter 3 begins by linking media images with criminal behavior. It discusses how rap music—specifically gangsta rap—and heavy metal music have recently been criticized for poisoning the minds of our youth. Indeed, there has been movement among several political groups to censor these types of music. This discussion question requires you to go to the library and gather research that examines whether heavy metal and rap music cause juvenile delinquency. After gathering this information, choose one of the two positions below and argue your position:

   ■ Heavy metal and rap music should be censored.
   ■ Heavy metal and rap music should not be censored.

3. Choose one of the theories discussed in Chapter 3. Assume that research has established that this theory has unequivocally identified the cause of crime. Now that you know what causes crime, what changes would you recommend in the criminal justice system and society to eliminate the crime problem in America? Be sure to discuss the theory and the changes that you would recommend. (The discussion in the text of each general type of theory and social policy would be helpful here. For example, if you were to argue that biology provides a definitive explanation for crime, the section on social policy and biological theories would be a good starting point for completing this assignment.)

CRIMINAL LAW

CHAPTER SUMMARY

Imagine our society without laws. How would order be maintained? How would individuals be protected from harm? How would society be protected? Law provides these protections, insulating society from mass chaos. The text discusses many different areas of law in Chapter 4, including the historical sources of modern law, the purposes of law, the different types of law, and the elements of a criminal law violation.

Where does our modern law come from? The text discusses several sources of modern law, beginning with the Code of Hammurabi, one of the oldest codes of law, which established property and other rights. Another source of modern law is early Roman law, including the basic rules related to family, religion, and economics contained in the Twelve Tables. The major source of our modern criminal law is common law, developed in England and now adopted in most English-speaking countries. Common law is the traditional body of unwritten legal precedents created by judges in their everyday practices. The United States Constitution, created at the federal Constitutional Convention in the late 1700s, is another important source of modern law. It is the final authority on questions pertaining to the rights of individuals, and it gives the federal and state governments the power to create laws and to limit punishments.

Chapter 4 also explains why we have laws. One of the primary purposes of law is to preserve and maintain social order. Laws can also promote change in society or help society adapt to change. For example, laws have had to be created in response to the computer revolution. Many criminal laws were created to adapt to the rapid technological changes. Being able to create laws to adapt changes in society also provides an opportunity for certain groups to influence the structure of those laws to their benefit (a conflict theory of law), although Roscoe Pound argued that law created reflected the interests of the majority in society (a consensus theory of law).

The text also discusses different types of law. Criminal law, which is the focus of the book, is concerned with offenses against society. The criminal justice processing machinery in place to respond to crime in society operates according to criminal law. Chapter 4 also distinguishes criminal law from civil law. Civil law provides legal guidance regulating the relationships between individuals. An individual, however, could be charged under criminal law, but also sued civilly by the victim. Case law involves the decisions of courts that provide guiding principles to future decisions, and administrative law is the body of law that regulates industry, business, and individuals.

Chapter 4 also provides a discussion of general categories of crime. Specifically, it discusses five categories of violations: misdemeanors, felonies, offenses, treason, and inchoate offenses.

Finally, Chapter 4 discusses the elements of a criminal law violation. Let's walk a fact situation through the elements discussed.

Facts: Joan killed her husband by stabbing him with a kitchen knife. Joan had been frequently subjected to beatings by her husband, some resulting in her having to be hospitalized. Moreover, her husband had threatened to kill Joan on at least four prior occasions.

1. *Actus Reus.* The first element of a criminal law violation is that there has to be an act in violation of the law. Here, the act is the killing. If Joan stabbed her husband, but he survived, she could be charged with attempted murder. If Joan took steps to complete the murder but was unable to carry out her attempt, she could be charged with conspiracy to commit murder. If she approached another person and asked that person to commit a murder, she could be charged with solicitation to commit a murder.
2. *Mens Rea.* A guilty mind is the second element that has to be established. It is probably the most complex because it involves subjective evaluation of the mind. Should Joan be held to blame for this crime? Did Joan intend the consequences of her action?
3. Concurrence. The third element is the concurrence of the act and the intent. Joan's actions have to be linked with her intent.
4. Harm. The harm in this case, the death of another human being, is easily identified.
5. Causation. There has to be a link between the act and the harm. If Joan shot her husband and he survived for a month, but died later of complications related to a cancerous brain tumor, it would be difficult to convict Joan of murder because the act would not be linked to the harm.
6. Legality. There has to be a law on the books prohibiting the act in question. Murder is well defined in our law books.
7. Punishment. Not only must there be a law on the books, but that law must provide a punishment for the crime. Statutory punishments for murder are among the severest punishments available to judges.

Even if each of the elements are established, a defendant has the opportunity to raise defenses that could excuse their actions. The last part of Chapter 4 discusses such defenses. For example, Joan might argue that she committed the act in self-defense since she was a battered woman who thought her life was in danger. Personal, situational, procedural, and innovative defenses are discussed at the end of Chapter 4.

Personal defenses are based on some characteristic of the individual who is charged with the crime. Examples include age, insanity, involuntary intoxication, and unconsciousness. Defenses based upon circumstance take into consideration the situation surrounding the crime. Examples include self-defense, duress, entrapment, accident, mistake, necessity, provocation, consent, and alibi. Procedural defenses are defenses based on procedure, such as double jeopardy, collateral estoppel, selective prosecution, denial of speedy trial, and prosecutorial misconduct. Innovative defenses are similar to personal defenses, but are typically unique and emerging defenses. Examples include black rage, urban survival syndrome, defense of abuse, and police fraud.

LEARNING TIPS

MEMORY TECHNIQUES

You can enhance your memory by creating associations. Your memory stores information in patterns which make sense to you. When additional information is gathered, it will be recalled more effectively if stored near similar information. For example, if you learn about a prison with a rigorous working scheme, a way to better remember it is to connect it with another prison you know to have the same working scheme. If you visualize the two together, you are better able to remember them and their agendas.

ACRONYMS

To learn a series of facts, especially a lengthy series, utilize mnemonic acronyms. Acronyms are words which are formed through the first letters of a list of words. For example, ROR is an acronym for Released On Recognizance. Mnemonic devices can enhance the memorization of almost anything, from simple lists to learning a variety of criminal justice theorists.

KEY TERMS

Law: A rule of conduct, generally found enacted in the form of a statute, which proscribes and/or mandates certain forms of behavior. Statutory law is often the result of moral enterprise by interest groups which, through the exercise of political power, are successful in seeing their valuative perspectives enacted into law.

Statutory Law: Written or codified law. The "law on the books," as enacted by a governmental body or agency having the power to make laws.

Case Law: That body of judicial precedent, historically built upon legal reasoning and past interpretations of statutory laws, which serves as a guide to decision making, especially in the courts.

Common Law: A body of unwritten judicial opinion which was based upon customary social practices of Anglo-Saxon society during the Middle Ages.

Jurisprudence: The philosophy of law; the science and study of the law.

Jural Postulates: Propositions developed by Roscoe Pound which hold that the law reflects shared needs without which members of society could not coexist. Pound's jural postulates are often linked to the idea that the law can be used to engineer the social structure to ensure certain kinds of outcomes (such as property rights embodied in the law of theft do in capitalistic societies).

> Example: One of Pound's jural postulates was that men and women must be able to assume that no intentional aggression will be committed against them.[1]

Consensus Theory of Law: Law is the product of shared social needs experienced by the majority of members in society.

Conflict Theory of Law: Law is the tool of powerful individuals and groups acting in their own interests.

Mala in se: Acts which are wrong in themselves.

> Example: Murder, rape, theft, and arson are *mala in se* offenses.

Mala prohibita: Acts which are wrong only because they are prohibited by the law.

> Example: Statutes that define drug use, prostitution, and gambling as criminal offenses are mala prohibita offenses.

Criminal Law: That branch of modern law which concerns itself with offenses committed against society, members thereof, their property, and the social order.

---

[1] Roscoe Pound, *Social Control Through Law.* Hamden, Connecticut, Archon Books, 1968.

Crime: An act committed in violation of a law forbidding or commanding it for which the possible penalties for an adult upon conviction include incarceration, for which a corporation can be penalized by fine or forfeit, or for which a juvenile can be adjudged delinquent or transferred to criminal court for prosecution.

> Example: Darrin Jackson committed a crime when he scared a 65-year-old man to death. Darrin robbed the victim of his wallet, which caused him to have a heart attack and die.

Penal Code: The written, organized, and compiled form of the criminal laws of the jurisdiction.

Precedent: A legal principle which operates to ensure that previous judicial decisions are authoritatively considered and incorporated into future cases.

Civil Law: That portion of modern law which regulates contracts and other obligations involving primarily personal interests.

> Example: Stella Liebeck won a 2.9 million dollar civil award after suing McDonald's for spilling coffee in her lap.[2]

Tort: A private or civil wrong or injury. A breach of duty to an individual that results in harm to that person.

Administrative Law: The body of regulations which have been created by governments to control the activities of industry, business, and individuals.

Misdemeanor: An offense punishable by incarceration, usually in a local confinement facility, for a period of which the upper limit is prescribed by statute in a given jurisdiction, typically limited to a year or less.

> Example: trespass, simple assault

Felony: A criminal offense punishable by death or by incarceration in a prison facility for at least a year.

> Example: murder, rape, robbery

Treason: "a U.S. citizen's actions to help a foreign government overthrow, make war against, or seriously injure the United States." Source: Daniel Oran, *Oran's Dictionary of the Law* (St. Paul, MN: West Publishing, 1983).

Espionage: The "gathering, transmitting or losing" of information related to the national defense in such a manner that the information becomes available to enemies of the United States and may be used to their advantage. Source: Henry Campbell Black, Joseph R. Nolan, and Jacqueline M. Nolan-Haley, *Black's Law Dictionary*, 6th ed. (St. Paul, MN: West Publishing, 1990), p. 24.

Inchoate Offense: One not yet completed. Also, an offense which consists of an action or conduct which is a step toward the intended commission of another crime.

> Example: Bob and Sam planned to kill their parents by poisoning them. They bought arsenic to serve to their parents with dinner. A police officer discovered the plan before Bob and Sam were able to carry it out. Both could be charged with conspiracy, an inchoate offense.

Actus Reus: An act in violation of the law.

Mens Rea: The state of the mind which accompanies a criminal act. Also, guilty mind.

Corpus delicti: The "body of the crime."

---

[2] "Tort Reform: The Price of Justice; Are Megabucks Lawsuits Ruining the Country?" *The Atlanta Journal and Constitution*, May 21, 1995.

Defenses: (to a criminal charge) Includes claims based upon personal, special, and procedural considerations that the defendant should not be held accountable for their actions, even though they may have acted in violation of the criminal law.

> Comment: What should we do with defendants whose criminal behavior in America would be acceptable behavior in their native culture? For example, when a Japanese woman living in this country discovered that her husband had a mistress, she drowned her two children and tried to commit suicide by drowning herself. She was saved, however. The Japanese do not think suicide is sinful, but leaving one's children behind by committing suicide is wrong. This woman was charged with the murder of her two children, and her defense attorney tried unsuccessfully to raise a cultural defense, saying the woman was culturally unable to leave living children.[3]

Insanity Defense: A personal defense which claims that the person charged with a crime did not know what they were doing or that they did not what they were doing was wrong.

> Example: A woman strangles her child, but believed she was wringing out a dish cloth. Her defense would be insanity and she would argue that she did not know what she was doing.

Self-defense: The protection of oneself or one's property from unlawful injury or the immediate risk of unlawful injury; the justification for an act which would otherwise constitute an offense, that the person who committed it reasonably believed that the act was necessary to protect self or property from immediate danger.

Entrapment: An inducement to crime by agents of enforcement.

PRACTICE TEST QUESTIONS

MULTIPLE CHOICE

4-1. Which of the following is an early set of legal principles, engraved in stone, and established to ensure property and other rights?
   a. Early Roman law
   b. The Ten Commandments
   c. The Code of Hammurabi
   d. The Magna Carta
   e. The United States Constitution

4-2. _____ law refers to a traditional body of unwritten legal precedents created through everyday practice and supported by court decisions.
   a. Common
   b. Administrative
   c. Civil
   d. Conflict
   e. Criminal

4-3. Murder, robbery, and drug offenses would all be defined as crimes under what branch of modern law?
   a. common
   b. administrative
   c. civil
   d. conflict
   e. criminal

---

[3] "Courts Ambivalent to Cultural Defenses," *United Press International*, December 7, 1987.

4-4. _____ law results from legislative action and is thought of as the "law of the land" or the "law on the books."
   a. Statutory
   b. Substantive
   c. Procedural
   d. Administrative
   e. Case

4-5. Tax laws, health codes, and restrictions on pollution are examples of what type of law?
   a. civil law
   b. criminal law
   c. administrative law
   d. procedural law
   e. natural law

4-6. Which of the following is a procedural defense?
   a. double jeopardy
   b. infancy
   c. duress
   d. mistake of fact
   e. urban survival syndrome

4-7. _____ is a Latin term meaning "the body of the crime."
   a. *Stare decisis*
   b. *Corpus delicti*
   c. *Actus reus*
   d. *Mens rea*
   e. *Sindee who*

4-8. A woman attempts to break into a home. Once she is in the home, she is confronted by the family dog Spike, a Rottweiler, who corners her. When the homeowner gets home from work and sees what Spike has in his possession, she quickly calls the police who apprehend the suspect. Based on these facts, the woman who broke into the home could be charged with _____
   a. burglary.
   b. attempted burglary.
   c. conspiracy to commit burglary.
   d. nothing, she did not commit a crime.

4-9. Which of the following elements of crime means "guilty mind?"
   a. *actus reus*
   b. *mens rea*
   c. concurrence
   d. harm
   e. causation

4-10. Which of the following is not a personal defense?
   a. infancy
   b. insanity
   c. involuntary intoxication
   d. self-defense
   e. unconsciousness

TRUE–FALSE

_____ 4-11. *Mala prohibita* crimes, such as drug use, are wrong in themselves.

_____ 4-12. A consensus theory of law states that law is the product of shared social needs experienced by the majority of members in society.

_____ 4-13. A basic distinction between criminal and civil law is that criminal acts injure individuals and society as a whole.

_____ 4-14. Misdemeanors are generally less serious than felonies.

_____ 4-15. Laws are only binding from the date of creation.

_____ 4-16. The Durham Rule states that a person is not guilty of a crime if, at the time of the crime, they didn't know what they were doing or didn't know that what they were doing was wrong.

_____ 4-17. Procedural defenses related to circumstances surrounding the crime and situational defenses are based upon some characteristic of the individual charged with a crime.

_____ 4-18. Contract law is the body of regulations which have been created by governments to control the economic activities of industry, business, and individuals.

_____ 4-19. Treason is the gathering, transmitting, or losing of information related to the national defense in such a manner that the information becomes available to enemies of the United States and may be used to their advantage.

_____ 4-20. Insanity is a legal definition and not a psychiatric one.

MATCHING

a. felony
b. *mens rea*
c. Durham Rule
d. *McNaughten* Rule
e. collateral estoppel
f. Black rage
g. conflict theory
h. consensus theory
i. misdemeanor
j. inchoate offense

_____ 4-21. States that law is the tool of powerful individuals and groups acting in their own interests.

_____ 4-22. Holds that a person is not guilty of a crime if, at the time of the crime, the person either didn't know what he/she was doing, or didn't know that what he/she was doing was wrong.

_____ 4-23. An offense which consists of an action or conduct which is a step toward the intended commission of another crime.

_____ 4-24. An offense punishable by incarceration, usually in a local confinement facility, for a period of which the upper limit is prescribed by statute in a given jurisdiction, typically limited to a year or less.

_____ 4-25. An innovative defense.

_____ 4-26. States that a person is not criminally responsible for their behavior if their illegal actions were the result of some mental disease or defect.

_____ 4-27. The theory of law based on the writings of Roscoe Pound.

_____ 4-28. A criminal offense punishable by death or by incarceration in a prison facility for at least a year.

_____ 4-29. A term that literally means "guilty mind."

_____ 4-30. A procedural defense.

DISCUSSION EXERCISES

1. Presented below are a number of case descriptions. If you, a defense attorney, were asked to take each of these cases, what would you recommend as the best defense to use? Why? (Refer to Table 4-2 in the book for assistance.)

a. Art Kapser and John Gelbor were good friends and coworkers. After work, Art and John went bowling. After John picked up a spare in the seventh frame, the two got into an argument on proper scoring of a spare. John punched Art in the face, knocking him to the floor and screaming "If you don't shut up, I will kill you." Art left the bowling alley, but returned with a .38 caliber revolver and shot John in the back, killing him instantly. He was charged with murder. What could Art use as a defense?

b. Kellie Koser attended a college party. One of the partygoers gave her a beer. She drank it, not knowing that the beer contained a sedative. She got tired quickly, and decided to drive home. She fell asleep at the wheel and killed a bicyclist. She was charged with murder. What could Kellie use as a defense?

c. Shelly Morrison and Todd Rutlow both drive the same model of pickup truck. Both trucks are black with a white pinstripe, both have red fuzzy dice hanging from the rear view mirror, and both have a bumper sticker with the slogan "Peace is Possible." Moreover, both leave their keys in the ignition when it is parked. Shelly, after completing a long day of Christmas shopping, got into a black truck and drove away. She did not know it was Todd's truck. Police quickly apprehended Shelly and charged her with motor vehicle theft. What would you recommend as a defense?

d. Charles Shuter was charged with raping his 14-year-old daughter. The prosecutor also charged the mother with conspiracy to commit rape because she knew about the rape and bought condoms for her husband to use when committing the crime. The mother claims she did not contact the police because the husband threatened to kill her. What would you recommend as a defense?

e. When Marnee Diaz lost her job, she found that she couldn't keep up with her bills. In order to put food on the table, she began committing bank robberies. What would you recommend as a defense?

f. Carol Smith is addicted to crack, but enrolled herself in a drug treatment program to control her addiction. An undercover police officer joined the same program to get information about drug suppliers. He got friendly with Ms. Smith and asked her to buy him some crack. She refused on four occasions. On the fifth occasion, however, she brought him one rock of crack cocaine. She was arrested for drug possession. What defense would you recommend?

g. Jason Jenser was a heavy drinker. Whenever he drank, he beat his lover, Bill. He frequently put a gun to Bill's head, threatened to kill him, and caused him numerous physical injuries. Bill tried to leave, but Jenser threatened him with physical violence, so he stayed. That same evening, while Jenser was sleeping, Bill picked up a shotgun and killed him. What defense would you recommend?

2. It would be helpful for you to refer to the discussion of the insanity defense in the text before tackling this discussion exercise.

The insanity defense is one of the more controversial and complex defenses available to defendants. It is controversial because the public thinks that defendants are excused from punishment when found not guilty by reason of insanity. The complexity lies in its link between the medical and legal professions.

Consider the legal implications of the following case: Tom Smith had recently escaped from a mental hospital when picked up by a concerned motorist. At a highway rest area, Tom killed the motorist by strangulation. He was charged with murder. On two prior occasions, Tom was found not guilty by reason of insanity for two murders.

The medical implications are that Tom has the IQ of about a 10-year-old child. He has a fifteen-year history of mental illness, dating back to his return from Vietnam. Tom suffers from post traumatic stress disorder, and is unable to recover from the horrors he experienced in war. He is delusional. When the motorist who picked him up began listening to Grateful Dead rock music, Tom strangled him because he thought the motorist was the Antichrist.

The prosecution had no trouble establishing the elements of the crime. The defense attorneys used an insanity defense (irresistible impulse test), claiming that Tom belongs in a mental hospital not a maximum security prison. If you were the judge in this case, what would you decide? Should Tom be punished as a criminal or treated as a person with a mental illness? Explain your rationale.

C H A P T E R

POLICING: HISTORY AND STRUCTURE

CHAPTER SUMMARY

Chapter 5 begins with a discussion of the historical development of police agencies in England and America. It discusses the similarities of the historical evolution of policing in England with historical changes in American policing. An organized police response to social problems in England did not occur until the 1700s. Prior to that time, a posse, led by a **shire reeve** or *comes stabuli,* would respond to assist victims when harmed. The English police started to evolve in the 1700s when **Henry Fielding** became the magistrate of the Bow Street Region of London. Later, under the guidance of **Sir Robert Peel**, the **New Police** (or the **Metropolitan Police**) was formed in 1829, and has been acknowledged as the world's first modern police force. Characteristics of the New Police force can still be found in English and American police forces. For example, the New Police operated under the belief that is was possible to discourage crime by patrolling the streets; wore uniforms to make themselves accessible to the public; and structured their departments much the same as a military organization.

American policing evolved similarly, and early police departments, such as those organized in New York City, Boston, and Cincinnati, studied Peel's New Police when deciding structure and police response. However, police departments in America also evolved to address the special and unique concerns of the country, such as managing the Western frontier.

American police departments have evolved considerably over the years, relying recently on scientific research studies when deciding how to respond to crime most effectively. The text discusses important research studies that have had a tremendous impact on the current structure and philosophy of police departments, such as the **Kansas City Preventive Patrol Experiment**. This experiment, conducted in the mid-

1970s, tested (among other things) the effectiveness of preventive patrol in deterring crime and making citizens feel safe. The results from this study indicated that the number of officers on preventive patrol did not have a deterrent effect on preventable crimes and did not make citizens feel safe. These findings have forced police departments to alter how they use police officers on patrol, employing such innovative police strategies as directed patrol and split-force patrol.

Chapter 5 also provides a discussion of the decentralized structure of policing in America, highlighting differences among federal, state, local, and privately owned law enforcement agencies. Federal law enforcement agencies are responsible for enforcing federal law violations. Although there are many different agencies with federal law enforcement responsibilities, the text describes in detail the three largest and best known: the **Federal Bureau of Investigation**, the **Drug Enforcement Administration**, and the **U.S. Marshals Service**.

Chapter 5 also discusses the responsibilities of state and local law enforcement agencies. State police agencies, whether centralized or decentralized, are responsible for patrolling state highways and conducting statewide criminal investigations. Officers that work for local law enforcement agencies have a more diverse job description when compared to federal and state officers. For example, the text discusses the diverse responsibilities of officers that work for the New York City police department. It also discusses the wide diversity in size and structure of local law enforcement agencies.

Chapter 5 concludes with a discussion of the growing private law enforcement industry. Indeed, the author notes that the number of individuals employed in private security is higher than the other levels combined. Although the primary concern of the book is on how local, state, and federal police respond to crime, discussion of private policing is important because of the growing influence of private security on criminal justice and the overlap between public and private security agencies.

LEARNING TIPS

TESTS

Managing review time is essential for test preparation. Instant reviews, which should occur either directly after the class meeting or during your assigned readings, start the learning and memorization process. Weekly reviews should be more focused than longer reviews. Lastly, final reviews are the most in-depth reviews. They should be conducted within the week prior to the exam. Final reviews help demonstrate the big picture and further understanding of the information provided during the entire class. Used together, instant, weekly, and final reviews provide the foundation for successful test preparation.

FLASH CARDS

Flash cards are extremely beneficial because they allow for studying on the go. Write key words, vocabulary, phrases, names, or theories on one side of a 3 x 5 card and write the answer on the other. This is especially helpful for the numerous legal cases that are included in the text. Study with the flash cards at home, on the bus, waiting for classes to begin, or whenever you have spare time.

BEFORE THE TEST

Be sure to arrive early for exams. This will allow for relaxation and general preparation. Avoid talking to other students about their test preparation. This will only cause more anxiety. Listen to all instructions while the exam is being distributed. As redundant as it may seem, read the directions twice. You may lose significant points for not following the most simple instructions. Before beginning, if necessary, take a minute to release all test anxieties and to relax your mind.

KEY TERMS

Comes Stabuli: Nonuniformed mounted early law enforcement officers in medieval England. Early police forces were small and relatively unorganized, but made effective use of local resources in the formation of posses, the pursuit of offenders, and the like.

New Police (Metropolitan Police): Formed in England in 1829 and commanded by Sir Robert Peel. Peel's police became the model for modern-day police forces throughout the Western world.

Scientific Police Management: The application of social scientific techniques to the study of police administration for the purpose of increasing effectiveness, reducing citizen complaints, and enhancing the efficient use of available resources.

Directed Patrol: A police management strategy designed to increase the productivity of patrol officers through the application of scientific analysis and evaluation of patrol techniques.

> Example: If a police department discovered that a large number of drunk driving offenses occurred on weekend and evening hours at a two-block location, that department might increase the number of officers patrolling this area during weekend and evening hours to increase the deterrent effect of patrol and the likelihood of apprehending law violators.

Sheriff: The elected chief officer of a county law enforcement agency, usually responsible for enforcement in unincorporated areas and for the operation of the county jail.

Private Protective Agencies: Independent or proprietary commercial organizations which provide protective services to employers on a contractual basis. Private security agencies, which already employ about half as many people as public law enforcement, are expected to experience substantial growth over the next few decades.

PRACTICE TEST QUESTIONS

MULTIPLE CHOICE

5-1. Who is most closely associated with London's Bow Street Runners?
   a. Sir Robert Peel
   b. Patrick Murphy
   c. Jonathan Wild
   d. Henry Fielding

5-2. Which of the following was not characteristic of the "New Police"?
   a. They believed that is was possible to deter crime by preventive patrol.
   b. They were uniformed.
   c. They resembled a military organization and adopted a military administrative style.
   d. They occupied fixed posts throughout the city awaiting a public outcry.

5-3. Which of the following aspects of police work is the "backbone of policing"?
   a. patrol
   b. investigation
   c. management
   d. administration
   e. crime prevention

5-4. Which of the following scientific police studies found that offenders who were arrested were less likely to commit repeat offenses than those handled in some other fashion?
   a. Kansas City Preventive Patrol Experiment
   b. Minneapolis Domestic Violence Experiment
   c. Newport News Problem-Oriented Policing Experiment
   d. Newark Foot Patrol Experiment
   e. New York City Police Department's Cadet Corps Study

5-5. Which Federal Law Enforcement Agency has the responsibility of prison transportation and custody, the pursuit and arrest of fugitives, security in federal courts, personal protection of judges, and the guarding of federal witnesses?
   a. Federal Bureau of Investigation
   b. Drug Enforcement Administration
   c. U.S. Marshals Service
   d. U.S. Customs Service
   e. None of the above

5-6. Which Federal Law Enforcement Agency includes law enforcement, counterintelligence, investigative support, law enforcement services, and direction, control, and administration within its mission statement?
   a. Federal Bureau of Investigation
   b. Drug Enforcement Administration
   c. U.S. Marshals Service
   d. U.S. Customs Service
   e. None of the above

5-7. A(n) _____ is responsible for the operation of a county jail.
   a. United States marshal
   b. state highway patrol officer
   c. sheriff
   d. uniformed patrol officer

5-8. *Shire reeve* means
   a. mounted officer.
   b. leader of the county.
   c. police chief.
   d. attorney general.

5-9. Who was responsible for starting the world's first modern police force?
   a. Henry Fielding
   b. Sir Robert Peel
   c. "Wild Bill" Hickok
   d. Richard Mayne
   e. Dorothy Moses Schultz

5-10. All of the following are reasons for the growth of private security in America except:
   a. an increase in fear of crime.
   b. an increase in crimes in the workplace.
   c. the fiscal crisis of the states.
   d. public police agencies requesting assistance from private agencies.

TRUE–FALSE

_____ 5-11. Early American police departments were structured according to the British model.

_____ 5-12. *Comes stabuli* is a Latin term which means a uniformed leader of the county.

_____ 5-13. Results from the Kansas City Preventive Patrol experiment indicate that officers on patrol deter crimes such as burglary and robbery and make citizens feel safe.

_____ 5-14. A centralized state law enforcement agency, such as the Pennsylvania State Police, combines the tasks of major criminal investigations with highway patrol.

_____ 5-15. There are more people employed in private security than all local, state, and federal police agencies combined.

_____ 5-16. The New York City Police Department has been hailed as the world's first modern police force.

_____ 5-17. The scientific police study undertaken in Newport News, Virginia, examined whether existing gun laws could reduce gun crimes.

_____ 5-18. The Federal Bureau of Investigation is probably the most famous law enforcement agency in this country.

_____ 5-19. Early in his career, J. Edgar Hoover was personally responsible for apprehending the infamous criminal Jonathan Wild.

_____ 5-20. Directed patrol is a police management strategy designed to increase the productivity of patrol officers through the application of scientific analysis and evaluation of patrol techniques.

MATCHING

a. directed patrol
b. Kansas City Preventive Patrol Experiment
c. Minneapolis Domestic Violence Experiment
d. Drug Enforcement Administration
e. Shire Reeve
f. New Police

g. split-force patrol
h. Kansas City Gun Experiment
i. *comes stabuli*
j. United States Marshals Service
k. Federal Bureau of Investigation
l. Wells Fargo Agency

_____ 5-21. The oldest federal law enforcement agency.

_____ 5-22. Term that means "leader of the county."

_____ 5-23. Also known as the *Metropolitan Police*.

_____ 5-24. The federal law enforcement agency which compiles the *Uniform Crime Reports*.

_____ 5-25. A police management strategy designed to increase the productivity of patrol officers through the application of scientific analysis and evaluation of patrol techniques.

_____ 5-26. The federal law enforcement agency that focuses on international and domestic drug trafficking.

_____ 5-27. A term which means *mounted officer*.

_____ 5-28. The first scientifically engineered social experiment to test the impact of the use of arrest upon crime.

_____ 5-29. The study that found that vigorous enforcement of gun laws could reduce crime.

_____ 5-30. The study credited with beginning the now-established tradition of scientific police evaluation.

DISCUSSION EXERCISES

1. Try to discover all law enforcement agencies that have responsibilities for carrying out law enforcement duties in the county where the university you attend is located. List these agencies and law enforcement responsibilities. Do any of the agencies have responsibilities that overlap? What changes would you suggest to effectively use the personnel resources?

2. You have just been hired as the police chief of a small (about 45 officers) department. You were hired because you promised the mayor and city council that you could reduce the number of street crimes by using more officers on location-oriented patrol. The city council has agreed to provide the department with funds to hire 16 new police officers to be used for location-oriented patrol. However, this money will only be provided to the department after you discuss how you will document whether location-oriented patrol deters crime. Specifically, the city council wants you to design a research study, not unlike the Kansas City Preventive Patrol Experiment, to evaluate the effectiveness of location-oriented patrol. Discuss your research design, including how you would use the new officers in the study, length of time of the study, and beat selection. (Be sure to read the discussion on the Kansas City Preventive Patrol section in the text.)

POLICE MANAGEMENT

CHAPTER SUMMARY

Chapter 6 discusses four different areas that affect police management: policing styles, officer discretion, contemporary concerns, and professionalism and ethics.

Police departments have unique policing styles formed in response to community and organizational factors. Three types of policing styles, developed by James Q. Wilson, were discussed in Chapter 6. First, police officers employed in **Watchman Style** departments are most concerned with order maintenance. These officers possess a considerable amount of discretion to resolve situations. Second, police officers in **Legalistic Style** departments are expected to enforce the letter of the law, meaning that their discretion to use a non-enforcement response is limited. Moreover, these officers are likely to ignore other disruptive behaviors. Third, an officer in a **Service Style** department is most concerned with helping citizens rather than strictly applying the letter of the law. These officers would be familiar with community resources, using these resources to help solve community and individual problems.

Many police departments are moving to the Service Style approach, utilizing what is popularly known as community policing strategies. **Community policing** is a strategy where police departments develop community relationships and solicit citizen assistance in solving problems. The current movement towards community policing has its roots in the **police-community relations** programs advocated in the 1960s as well as the **team policing** ideas of the 1970s. The text discusses several examples of community policing programs within this chapter, such as Houston's DART program, Chicago's Alternative Policing Strategy, and New York City's Community Police Officer Program.

Chapter 6 also introduces the idea of individual officer **discretion**. Despite the potential influence of department styles, individual officers possess an opportunity to make alternative choices when enforcing the law. While working the streets, officers are not directly supervised by superiors, providing them with discretion to informally or formally resolve incidents. The text describes potential factors that might influence how officers use discretion, including the background of the officer, characteristics of the suspect, community interests, and pressures from the victim.

One powerful influence on an officer's use or misuse of discretion is the **police culture**. New recruits are molded by the police culture, as supervisors and other officers teach rookie officers the informal policies of the department. Thus, there are two sets of rules that new police officers must learn and follow. The first set of rules include those formal departmental policies and legal constraints that the officer learns in the training academy. The second set of rules involves the informal socialization that takes place as officers interact with older, experienced officers who teach how formal rules get interpreted. For example, experienced officers might explain to a new recruit that accepting free meals or bribes is expected in the department, despite departmental policy clearly prohibiting such behavior. The text discusses such activities in the section on police corruption, noting its historical pervasiveness.

Other police issues discussed in Chapter 6 include drug testing of recruits and random testing of hired employees. In addition, the dangers of police work are discussed, including exposure to blood evidence that might contain disease, deadly force, police stress, and others.

The author concludes by discussing issues of **professionalism** and **ethics**; important tools in addressing concerns associated with issues such as corruption. The accreditation of police departments, increasing educational standards, and improving the recruitment and selection of officers are changes being made to address problem areas of policing.

LEARNING TIPS

ON EXAMS, GO WITH YOUR FIRST INSTINCT

It is usually best to stick with your first choice on the objective questions such as true/false and multiple choice. Avoid going against your first instinct unless you are convinced that your second answer is correct upon further reflection or deduction.

KEY TERMS

Police Management: The administrative activities of controlling, directing, and coordinating police personnel, resources, and activities in the service of crime prevention, the apprehension of criminals and the recovery of stolen property, and the performance of a variety of regulatory and helping services.

Watchman Style: A style of policing which is marked by a concern for order maintenance. This style of policing is characteristic of lower class communities where informal police intervention into the lives of residents is employed in the service of keeping the peace.

Legalistic Style: A style of policing which is marked by a strict concern with enforcing the precise letter of the law. Legalistic departments, however, may take a "hands-off" approach to otherwise disruptive or problematic forms of behavior which are not violations of the criminal law.

Service Style: A style of policing which is marked by a concern with helping rather than strict enforcement. Service-oriented agencies are more likely to take advantage of community resources, such as drug treatment programs, than are other types of departments.

Police-Community Relations (PCR): An area of police activity which stresses the need for the community and the police to work together effectively and emphasizes the notion that the police derive their legitimacy from the community they serve. PCR began to be of concern to many police agencies in the 1960s and 1970s.

> Example: Officer Friendly programs, where police officers talk to school children about safety issues, Police Athletic Leagues, and Midnight Basketball Leagues are all examples of community relations programs.

Team Policing: The reorganization of conventional patrol strategies into "an integrated and versatile police team assigned to a fixed district." Source: Sam Souryal, *Police Administration and Management* (St. Paul, MN: West Publishing Co., 1977), p. 261.

Community Policing: A collaborative effort between the police and the community that identifies problems of crime and disorder and involves all elements of the community in the search for solutions to these problems.

> Example: The police department in Detroit uses storefront police stations to encourage the public to interact with the police.

Strategic Policing: A style of policing which retains the traditional police goal of professional crime fighting, but enlarges the enforcement target to include nontraditional kinds of criminals, such as serial offenders, gangs and criminal associations, drug distribution networks, and sophisticated white-collar and computer criminals. Strategic policing generally makes use of innovative enforcement techniques, including intelligence operations, undercover stings, electronic surveillance, and sophisticated forensic methods.

Problem-Solving Policing (also called *Problem-Oriented Policing*): A style of policing which assumes that many crimes are caused by existing social conditions within the community and that crimes can be controlled by uncovering and effectively addressing underlying social problems. Problem-solving policing makes use of other community resources, such as counseling centers, welfare programs, and job training facilities. It also attempts to involve citizens in the job of crime prevention through education, negotiation, and conflict management.

Discretion: The exercise of choice, by enforcement agents, in the disposition of suspects, in the carrying out of official duties, and in the application of sanctions.

> Example: When stopping a motorist for speeding, an officer has a number of discretionary decisions to make. She might ask the driver to exit the vehicle before approaching it, she might question the driver and let her go with a warning, or she might write the driver a ticket.

Police Culture (also *Subculture*): A particular set of values, beliefs, and acceptable forms of behavior characteristic of American police, with which the police profession strives to imbue new recruits. Socialization into the police subculture commences with recruit training and is ongoing thereafter.

Police Working Personality: All aspects of the traditional values and patterns of behavior evidenced by police officers who have been effectively socialized into the police subculture. Characteristics of the police personality often extend to the personal lives of law enforcement personnel.

Corruption: Behavioral deviation from an accepted ethical standard.

> Example: A police officer found sleeping in a car, drinking on duty, or confiscating stolen property for their own use are all examples of corrupt police practices.

1983 Lawsuits: Civil suits brought under Title 42, Section 1983 of the United States Code, against anyone denying others of their constitutional rights to life, liberty, or property without due process of law.

Biven Action: The name given to civil suits, based upon the case of *Bivens v. Six Unknown Defendants*, brought against federal government officials for denial of the constitutional rights of others.

Police Ethics: The special responsibility for adherence to moral duty and obligation inherent in police work.

Police Professionalism: The increasing formalization of police work and the rise in public acceptance of the police which accompanies it.

PRACTICE TEST QUESTIONS

MULTIPLE CHOICE

6-1. Police officer Sally Kainer works in a department that she describes as being concerned with community problems. She has been encouraged by the department to develop ties with other community agencies, such as the local chapter of Big Brothers/Big Sisters, and to rely on them for assistance. Which of Wilson's policing styles is represented by the department that Sally works for?
   a. watchman style
   b. legalistic style
   c. service style
   d. paternalistic style

6-2. Which historical era of policing was characterized by close ties between police and public officials?
   a. political era
   b. reform era
   c. community problem solving era
   d. renaissance era

6-3. Which of Wilson's policing styles is becoming increasingly popular today?
   a. watchman style
   b. legalistic style
   c. service style
   d. paternalistic style

6-4. Of the three "corporate strategies" that guide American policing, which emphasizes an increased capacity to deal with crimes that are not well controlled by traditional methods?
   a. strategic policing
   b. problem-solving policing
   c. community policing
   d. corporation policing

6-5. All of the following are criticisms of community policing strategies except:
   a. not all police officers accept this new image of police work.
   b. goals of community policing are too narrowly defined.
   c. efforts to promote community policing can demoralize a department.
   d. all public officials are not ready to accept community policing.

6-6. Which of the following is not a factor that influences the discretionary decisions of individual officers?
   a. background of the officer
   b. pressures from crime victims
   c. departmental policy
   d. available alternatives
   e. all of the above are factors that might influence police discretion

6-7. Which of the following is a type of police corruption that occurs in order to further the organizational goals of law enforcement?
   a. occupational deviance
   b. abuse of authority
   c. meat eating
   d. grass eating

6-8. In which of the following types of incident are officers the most likely to be killed in the line of duty?
   a. disturbance calls
   b. traffic enforcement
   c. arrest situations
   d. accidents

6-9. Which style of policing is marked by a strict concern with enforcing the precise letter of the law?
   a. legalistic
   b. watchman
   c. service
   d. paternalistic

6-10. Neighborhood Watch programs, drug awareness workshops, and Project ID are all examples of
   a. police crime fighting activities.
   b. innovative police strategies.
   c. police-community relations programs.
   d. types of patrol strategies.

6-11. Which type of policing strategy reorganizes conventional patrol strategies into integrated and versatile police teams assigned to a fixed district?
   a. team policing
   b. community policing
   c. problem- solving policing
   d. strategic policing

6-12. Which corporate police strategy evolved from the reform era of the mid-1900s?
   a. strategic policing
   b. problem-solving policing
   c. community policing
   d. team policing

6-13. Which of the following U.S. Supreme Court cases specified the conditions under which deadly force could be used to apprehend a suspected felon?
   a. *Tennessee* v. *Garner*
   b. *Bivens* v. *Six Unknown Defendants*
   c. *Mapp* v. *Ohio*
   d. *Hunter* v. *Bryant*

TRUE–FALSE

_____ 6-14. Legalistic police agencies are more likely to take advantage of community resources, such as drug treatment programs, than are other types of departments.

_____ 6-15. Scholars argue that American policing has just started the political era of policing.

_____ 6-16. Meat-eating police corruption is the most common form of police deviance, involving mostly small bribes or relatively small services.

_____ 6-17. Officers have the widest range of discretionary decisions available to them when they respond to crimes of minor significance.

_____ 6-18. Formal academy training is far more important in determining how rookies will see police work than is their informal socialization into the police culture.

_____ 6-19. The reform era that characterized policing from the 1930s until the 1970s was characterized by pride in professional crime fighting.

_____ 6-20. Although many police departments have dramatically increased recruitment of ethnic minorities into policing, females are still substantially underrepresented.

_____ 6-21. A Watchman Style of policing is characteristic of lower-class communities where informal police intervention into the lives of residents is employed in the service of keeping the peace.

_____ 6-22. POST and FLETC were two of the first community policing programs started in America.

_____ 6-23. Individuals must have at least a 4-year college degree before applying to all police departments for employment.

MATCHING

a. community policing
b. team policing
c. police ethics
d. police professionalism
e. watchman style

f. service style
g. legalistic style
h. corruption
i. problem-solving policing
j. strategic policing

_____ 6-24. A style of policing which is marked by a concern for order maintenance.

_____ 6-25. An innovative police strategy thought to have originated in Aberdeen, Scotland.

_____ 6-26. These types of department may take a "hands-off" approach to otherwise disruptive or problematic forms of behavior which are not violations of the criminal law.

_____ 6-27. A strategy of policing which assumes that many crimes are caused by existing social conditions within the community and that crimes can be controlled by uncovering and effectively addressing underlying social problems.

_____ 6-28. A collaborative effort between the police and the community that identifies problems of crime and disorder and involves all elements of the community in the search for solutions to the problems.

_____ 6-29. The special responsibility for adherence to moral duty and obligation inherent in police work.

_____ 6-30. A style of policing which is marked by a concern with helping rather than strict enforcement.

_____ 6-31. Behavioral deviation from an accepted ethical standard.

_____ 6-32. The increasing formalization of police work and the rise in public acceptance of the police which accompanies it.

_____ 6-33. A strategy of policing which retains the traditional police goal of professional crime fighting, but enlarges the enforcement target to include nontraditional kinds of criminals.

DISCUSSION EXERCISES

1. In Chapter 6, the author acknowledges individual police officer discretion as an important aspect of policing, but also notes the potential dangers of having limited oversight of officers in most situations. Below are a number of examples, not uncommon in police work, where police officers have had to exercise discretion. After each example, discuss how you, as a police officer, would respond to the situation. There are no right answers, but be certain to justify your response with an explanation:

a. You are dispatched to a low income apartment complex. A man named Arnold, who is homeless and addicted to crack, refuses to leave the entrance area to the building. He allows those living in the building to enter and does not bother most. However, a tenant has called to complain and would like him removed. It is mid-winter, and the temperature is below freezing. As the responding officer, how would you use your discretion to respond to this situation? Why?

b. While on random preventive patrol in a high-crime neighborhood, you notice two young kids (you think they are about 8 or 9 years old), hanging around outside of a drug store. When you approach them they start acting very nervous. It is about 8 o'clock at night. As you talk to them, a third kid, same age, comes out of the store, followed by the cashier who tells you that the third kid has just tried to steal three candy bars. How would you respond to this situation? Justify your action.

c. While randomly patrolling a neighborhood, you observe a vehicle run a red light. While in pursuit, you also notice that the person is driving in a haphazard manner. After the person stops his vehicle, you discover that he is drunk. The person driving the car, however, is also your favorite uncle. How would you respond to this situation? How does your response differ from the previous two situations?

d. Your department has received a call from a citizen complaining that his next door neighbors have been fighting for the last two hours (it is 3:30 a.m.). When you knock on the door and announce that you are the police, the fighting abruptly stops. A male, about 24 years old, opens the door and apologizes for the disturbance and promises that they will be quiet. However, he will not allow you into the home to talk with the person that he was fighting with. How would you resolve this situation?

e. You and your partner are asked to respond to a vehicle illegally blocking traffic. After investigating the scene, you discover that the vehicle has been reported stolen and, when taking inventory of the contents of the vehicle, you note three pieces of expensive stereo equipment in the back section of the van. Your partner tells you not to inventory the stereo equipment, and he puts it into the trunk of the car. He drops the equipment off at home before concluding the day. What would you do about this situation? Why?

POLICING: LEGAL ASPECTS

CHAPTER SUMMARY

Chapter 7 examines the legal constraints on police behavior. It discusses how law enforcement agents are constrained by procedural law, highlighting the legal rules that affect the **search and seizure** of evidence, **arrest**, and **interrogation**.

When conducting investigations, law enforcement officers will rely heavily on physical evidence to substantiate criminal charges. The legal constraints on evidence collection are found in the **Fourth Amendment**. In general, law enforcement agents will get a **warrant** to search and seize evidence when they can demonstrate **probable cause** to a neutral magistrate (a judge). If probable cause is later found to have been lacking, any items seized would be excluded as evidence. *Weeks* v. *United States* established the **exclusionary rule** for federal cases; *Mapp* v. *Ohio* made this rule applicable to the states.

There are some exceptions to the requirement that law enforcement agents obtain a warrant before collecting evidence, although most of them require that the agent still establish probable cause. For example, if a police officer is legally in a place where they are allowed to be, then any contraband in *plain view* can be seized as evidence (*Harris* v. *United States*), although they could not move an object to put it into plain view (*U.S.* v. *Irizarry, Arizona* v. *Hicks*). Another exception is a search incident to an arrest. When arresting a suspect, law enforcement agents can search the person and any area in the immediate control of that person (*Chimel* v. *California, U.S.* v. *Rabinowitz*) without a warrant. Other exceptions include emergency situations, stop and frisk, concern for public safety, vehicle searches, and consent searches. Table 7-3 presents a complete list of exceptions to the exclusionary rule).

The probable cause standard also applies to the law of **arrest**. Law enforcement agents arrest, or obtain a warrant to arrest, a suspect when the facts cause a reasonable person to believe that a specific individual has committed a crime. There are, however, instances where police officers might question someone they suspect of committing a crime, but may not arrest. For example, a police officer might stop to question a suspicious-looking individual and do a quick pat-down search for weapons (*Terry* v. *Ohio*). If the citizen was able to dispel the concerns of the officer, then that person would be free to leave.

Chapter 7 concludes with a discussion of **interrogation**. Law enforcement agents can, and do, question citizens suspected of committing a crime, but they cannot conduct an interrogation before ensuring that the suspect is protected against self-incrimination. Courts have prohibited physically-coercive interrogation techniques when questioning suspects (*Brown* v. *Mississippi*). The privilege against self-incrimination does not preclude officers from using psychologically-coercive techniques to elicit confessions, as long as the suspect is informed of his/her rights prior to custodial interrogation (*Miranda* v. *Arizona*).

The Fourth and Fifth Amendments are the two most significant and controversial procedural constraints on police behavior. These constraints have evolved considerably over the last thirty years because of changes in the ideological makeup of the U.S. Supreme Court. For example, evidence obtained based on an invalid warrant can still be used when the officer was acting in '**good faith**' (*United States* v. *Leon*). Law enforcement agents can question suspects without reading them their Miranda rights when public safety is at risk (*New York* v. *Quarles*).

KEY TERMS

Illegally Seized Evidence: Evidence seized in opposition to the principles of due process as described by the Bill of Rights. Most illegally seized evidence is the result of police searches conducted without a proper warrant or of improperly conducted interrogations.

> Example: When a campus police officer walked into a dormitory room and opened a student's top desk drawer without a warrant and without probable cause, the three weapons seized were illegally obtained.

Exclusionary Rule: The understanding that incriminating information must be seized according to Constitutional specifications of due process or it will not be allowable as evidence in criminal trials.

Writ of Certiorari: An order by an appellate court specifying whether or not the court will review the judgment of a lower court.

Fruit-of-the-Poisoned-Tree Doctrine: A legal principle which excludes from introduction at trial any evidence eventually developed as a result of an originally illegal search or seizure.

> Example: When invited into Jay Honer's home, a police officer asked to use his bathroom. When in the bathroom, he opened a bathroom drawer and discovered many credit cards that he suspected were stolen. The officer did not have a warrant to conduct the search. Mr. Honer was arrested and while searching through his pockets, the officers found a small bag of marijuana. Mr. Honer was arrested for fraud and drug possession. However, since the search was conducted without a warrant, the credit cards would be consider illegally obtained evidence. In addition, the evidence seized in the search incident to the arrest would also be excluded as fruit-of-the-poisoned-tree.

Good Faith: A possible legal basis for an exception to the exclusionary rule. Law enforcement officers who conduct a search, or seize evidence on the basis of good faith (that is, where they believe they are operating according to the dictates of the law), and who later discover that a mistake was made, may still use, in court, evidence seized as the result of such activities.

Plain View: A legal term describing the ready visibility of objects which might be seized during a search by police in the absence of a search warrant specifying the seizure of the objects. In order for evidence in plain view to be lawfully seized, officers must have a legal right to be in the viewing area and must have cause to believe that the evidence is somehow associated with criminal activity.

> Example: When walking down an apartment corridor in response to a call for assistance, a police officer passes a door propped open by a box. In the box is a white pow-

dery substance that the officer suspects is cocaine. Since this evidence is in plain view, the officer would be able to seize it and not violate the Fourth Amendment.

Emergency Searches: Those searches conducted by the police without a warrant, which are justified on the basis of some immediate and overriding need—such as public safety, the likely escape of a dangerous suspect, or the removal or destruction of evidence.

Suspicionless Searches: Those searches conducted by law enforcement personnel without a warrant and without suspicion. These types of searches are only permissible if based upon an overriding concern for public safety.

Probable Cause: Refers to the necessary level of belief which would allow for police seizures of individuals and searches of dwellings, vehicles, and possessions. Probable cause can generally be found in a set of facts and circumstances which would cause a reasonable person to believe that a particular individual has committed a specific crime. Upon a demonstration of probable cause, magistrates will issue warrants authorizing law enforcement officers to effect arrests and conduct searches.

Search Incident to an Arrest: Those warrantless searches of arrested individuals which are conducted in order to ensure the safety of the arresting officer(s). Because individuals placed under arrest may be in the possession of weapons, courts have recognized the need for arresting officers to protect themselves by conducting an immediate and warrantless search of arrested individuals without the need for a warrant.

Arrest: Taking an adult or juvenile into physical custody by authority of law, for the purpose of charging the person with a criminal offense or a delinquent act or status offense. Technically, an arrest occurs whenever a person's freedom to leave is curtailed by a law enforcement officer.

Compelling Interest: A legal concept which provides a basis for suspicionless searches (urinalysis tests of train engineers, for example) when public safety is at issue. It is the concept upon which the U.S. Supreme Court cases of *Skinner* v. *Railway Labor Executives' Association* (1989) and *National Treasury Employees Union* v. *Von Rabb* (1989) turned. In those cases the Court held that public safety may provide a sufficiently compelling interest such that an individual's right to privacy can be limited under certain circumstances.

Interrogation: The information-gathering activities of police officers which involve the direct questioning of suspects. The actions of officers during suspect interrogation are constrained by a number of U.S. Supreme Court decisions, the first of which was *Brown* v. *Mississippi* (1936).

Inherent Coercion: Those tactics used by police interviewers which fall short of physical abuse, but which, nonetheless, pressure subjects to divulge information.

Psychological Manipulation: Manipulative actions by police interviewers, designed to pressure subjects to divulge information, which are based upon subtle forms of intimidation and control.

Miranda Warnings: The advisement of rights due criminal suspects by the police prior to the beginning of questioning. *Miranda* warnings were first set forth by the Court in the 1965 case of *Miranda* v. *Arizona.*

> Example: In general, suspects must be advised that they have a right to remain silent, that anything they say may be used against them, that they have a right to an attorney, and that if they cannot afford an attorney, one will be provided to them prior to custodial interrogation.

ECPA: An acronym for the Electronic Communications Privacy Act.

KEY CASES

Note that there are many other cases discussed in Chapter 7. The list below provides only a few of the most significant Fourth and Fifth Amendment cases.

Weeks v. *United States*: Evidence obtained by federal officers in violation of the Fourth Amendment, in federal prosecutions, will be excluded (see Exclusionary Rule).

> Example: Sheila Long was watching television in her apartment when officers from the Drug Enforcement Administration came through her screen door and went through her kitchen drawers. They found two kilograms of heroin, although they did not have a warrant. She was charged in violation of a federal drug statute. The evidence collected, however, would be excluded because of the decision in Weeks.

Mapp v. *Ohio*: The Fourth Amendment's Exclusionary Rule is applicable to the states through the Due Process Clause of the Fourteenth Amendment.

> Example: Sheila Long was watching television in her apartment when city police officers came through her screen door and went through her kitchen drawers. They found two kilograms of heroin, although they did not have a warrant. She was charged in violation of a state drug statute. The evidence collected, however, would be excluded because of the decision in Mapp.

Chimel v. *California*: A search, incident to a lawful arrest, is limited to the area in the immediate control or grabbing area of the suspect.

> Example: Sheila Long was arrested on a street corner for prostitution. The arresting officer searched her person, including her pockets, and discovered one rock of crack cocaine. The officer did not need a warrant to search her pockets because of the decision in Chimel.

United States v. *Leon*: Evidence obtained when exercising an invalid search warrant is still admissible if the officers were acting in good faith.

Harris v. *United States*: Objects falling in the plain view of an officer who has a right to be in the position to have that view are subject to seizure and may be introduced into evidence.

Terry v. *Ohio*: This case established the stop-and-frisk exception. A citizen can be briefly detained by law enforcement agents without probable cause when they have reasonable suspicion to believe the person has committed, or is about to commit, a crime. The agent can conduct a limited pat-down search of the suspect.

Carroll v. *United States*: A warrantless search of an automobile or other vehicle is valid if based upon probable cause that contraband is present.

Brown v. *Mississippi*: Law enforcement agents cannot use physically-coercive interrogation techniques to elicit confessions.

Miranda v. *Arizona*: Persons in custody must be advised of various warnings prior to being subjected to custodial interrogation.

New York v. *Quarles*: Public safety may justify an officer's questioning of a suspect when failing to read *Miranda* warnings.

Illinois v. *Perkins*: *Miranda* warnings are not required when a suspect does not believe that they are speaking to a law enforcement officer.

PRACTICE TEST QUESTIONS

MULTIPLE CHOICE

7-1. Which Constitutional amendment establishes legal boundaries for the search and seizure of evidence?
   a. First
   b. Second
   c. Fourth
   d. Fifth
   e. Eighth

7-2. Which Constitutional amendment establishes legal boundaries for the interrogation of suspects?
   a. First
   b. Second
   c. Fourth
   d. Fifth
   e. Eighth

7-3. Which of the following statements about the search and seizure of evidence is false?
   a. A warrantless search of an automobile is valid if it is based upon probable cause that contraband is present.
   b. Evidence viewed by an officer in plain view, when legally in a place where the officer is allowed to be, will not be excluded.
   c. Evidence illegally seized by the police cannot be used in a trial under most circumstances.
   d. In all circumstances, police officers must get a warrant in order to seize evidence.
   e. None of the above are false statements.

7-4. Which of the following legal principles excludes from introduction at trial any evidence obtained as a result of an originally illegal search or seizure?
   a. Good Faith Exception
   b. Fruit-of-the-Poisoned-Tree Doctrine
   c. Plain View Doctrine
   d. Public Safety Exception
   e. Compelling Interest Doctrine

7-5. Which U.S. Supreme Court case established the public safety exception to the *Miranda* Rule?
   a. *Mapp* v. *Ohio*
   b. *Weeks* v. *United States*
   c. *Brown* v. *Mississippi*
   d. *New York* v. *Quarles*
   e. *Leyra* v. *Denno*

7-6. Which U.S. Supreme Court case made the exclusionary rule applicable to the states?
   a. *Mapp* v. *Ohio*
   b. *Weeks* v. *United States*
   c. *Brown* v. *Mississippi*
   d. *New York* v. *Quarles*
   e. *Leyra* v. *Denno*

7-7. Which of the following U.S. Supreme Court cases does *not* involve the search of a vehicle?
  a. *Carroll* v. *United States*
  b. *South Dakota* v. *Opperman*
  c. *United States* v. *Ross*
  d. *United States* v. *Leon*
  e. *Florida* v. *Jimeno*

7-8. Which of the following U.S. Supreme Court cases does *not* involve police interrogation of suspects?
  a. *Miranda* v. *Arizona*
  b. *Escobedo* v. *Illinois*
  c. *Brown* v. *Mississippi*
  d. *Chimel* v. *California*
  e. *New York* v. *Quarles*

7-9. In which of the following situations would a law enforcement agent not be required to read a suspect the *Miranda* warnings?
  a. A police officer, disguised as a jail inmate, asks his cell mate "Did you commit the murder?"
  b. A police officer arrests a person for robbery and assault. When traveling to the police station for booking purposes, she asks the suspect, "What do you know about this robbery?"
  c. An off-duty police officer apprehends a purse snatcher. As the officer waits for a police car to transport the suspect, he asks, "How many purses have you stolen in the last month?"
  d. Jason Melo, convicted of rape and burglary, was serving time in a maximum-security prison. He was also a suspect in a murder investigation. In the visiting room of the prison, the detective asked Jason, "Did you murder your brother-in-law?"
  e. *Miranda* warnings would be required in all of the above situations.

7-10. In which of the following situations would a law enforcement officer be able to conduct a search if he or she did not have probable cause to do so?
  a. vehicle search
  b. search incident to an arrest
  c. suspicionless search
  d. none of the above

TRUE–FALSE

_____ 7-11. The current members of the United States Supreme Court are much more liberal-minded than in years past. Their liberalism is evidenced in court rulings expanding the rights of the defendants in cases such as *U.S.* v. *Leon* and *New York* v. *Quarles*.

_____ 7-12. Public safety may provide a sufficiently compelling interest such that an individual's right to privacy can be limited under certain circumstances.

_____ 7-13. A suspect can be forced to give fingerprints even when probable cause for an arrest does not exist.

_____ 7-14. A citizen can be briefly detained by law enforcement agents without probable cause when there is reasonable suspicion to believe the person has committed, or is about to commit, a crime.

_____ 7-15. If the police initiate an arrest in a person's home, because of the law regarding search incident to arrest, they could search the entire residence including opening drawers, closets, and trunks.

_____ 7-16. A *writ of certiorari* is the type of warrant that federal agents need to make an arrest.

_____ 7-17. Nontestimonial evidence, such as blood cells, cannot be seized as evidence under any circumstances.

_____ 7-18. The Electronic Communications Privacy Act specifically states that law enforcement officers cannot seize electronic communications in any circumstances.

_____ 7-19. Probable cause must be satisfactorily demonstrated by police officers under a written affidavit to a magistrate before a search warrant can be issued.

_____ 7-20. A police officer may, in certain emergencies, search a premises without a warrant.

MATCHING

a. *Weeks* v. *U.S.*
b. *Harris.* v. *U.S.*
c. *Mapp* v. *U.S.*
d. *New York* v. *Quarles*
e. *Minnesota* v. *Dickerson*
f. *Carroll* v. *U.S.*
g. *Silverthorne Lumber Co.* v. *U.S.*
h. *Miranda* v. *Arizona*
i. *U.S.* v. *Leon*
j. *Brown* v. *Mississippi*
k. *Terry* v. *Ohio*
l. *Aguilar* v. *Texas*
m. *Chimel* v. *California*
n. *Warden* v. *Hayden*

_____ 7-21. Case which articulated the fruit-of-the-poisoned-tree doctrine.

_____ 7-22. Case which established the good faith exception to the exclusionary rule.

_____ 7-23. Established a two-prong test to the effect that informant information could establish probable cause if both criteria were met.

_____ 7-24. Case which established the famous requirement of a police "rights advisement" of suspects.

_____ 7-25. Case which held that a search incident to an arrest is invalid when it goes beyond the person arrested and the area subject to that person's "immediate control."

_____ 7-26. Established the exclusionary rule in federal cases.

_____ 7-27. Case which established the stop-and-frisk exception to the exclusionary rule.

_____ 7-28. Case which placed limits on an officer's ability to seize evidence discovered during a pat down search.

_____ 7-29. Case which first recognized the need for emergency searches.

_____ 7-30. Case which made the exclusionary rule applicable to the states.

_____ 7-31. Case which established the public safety exception to the *Miranda* rule.

_____ 7-32. Case which first stated the plain view doctrine.

_____ 7-33. The first significant U.S. Supreme Court case involving an automobile.

DISCUSSION EXERCISES

1. In the following search and seizure situations, note whether you think the evidence seized would be excluded in a court of law.
   a. Police Officer A observes an automobile driving the wrong way on a one-way street. When the officer tries to stop the automobile, the driver flees, resulting in a high-speed chase. The chase ends when the suspect car crashes into a telephone poll.

Concerned that her car might ignite from a gas leak, the officer pulled the unconscious woman driver from the car. After placing the woman a safe distance from the car, he went back into the car to locate her purse for identification, at which time he found a knife covered in blood on the front seat. It was later discovered that the knife was used in the murder of another police officer. Should the knife be excluded? What court case(s) justifies your decision?

b. While off-duty and at a party, Police Officer A was asked by the homeowner to get some ice from his basement. Since the ice machine was not immediately apparent, the officer opened two doors. Behind door number two were six marijuana plants. The officer arrested the homeowner. Would you exclude the marijuana plants? What court case(s) justifies your decision?

c. Defendant A was suspected of selling stolen property from his dorm room. An undercover campus police officer knocked on Defendant A's door and, when answered, asked for an affordable radar detector. In response, Defendant A said that he just got two new ones last night. While in the room, the officer noticed various other items she suspected as being stolen. She bought one of the radar detectors and then used it to convince a judge to issue a search warrant of the room. Among the items confiscated in the search with the warrant were: four radar detectors; three television sets; two air-conditioning units; and 1,500 compact discs. Should this evidence be excluded? What court case(s) justifies your decision?

d. Police Officers A and B were observing a street corner for drug activity and noticed Defendant C selling drugs to Defendant D. These officers quickly arrived at the scene, but were only able to arrest Defendant D. Before they could handcuff him, Defendant D swallowed what appeared to them to be one balloon of heroin. Police Officer B forced his finger down Defendant D's throat, causing him to vomit. Among the extracted material was one balloon of heroin. Would this evidence be excluded? What court case(s) justifies your decision?

e. When executing a valid arrest warrant for an assault charge in Defendant A's home, Police Officer B seized a handgun in the search incident to the arrest. Alarmed that her life was in danger, Police Officer B made Defendant A lie with his face down to the floor and quickly perused three adjoining rooms. While walking through the kitchen, she noticed a pile of semi-automatic weapons on the table, which were seized as evidence. Should these weapons be excluded? What case(s) justifies your decision?

2. Recall from the discussion in Chapter 1 that justice requires a fair balance between individual and community interests. The U.S. Supreme Court's interpretation of the Fourth and Fifth Amendments provides an effective illustration of the difficulties in finding a fair balance. A public order advocate might argue that the exclusionary rule and the *Miranda* warnings have handcuffed the abilities of the police to effectively protect the community. An individual rights advocate, on the other hand, might argue that such changes have resulted in positive reform of the police and such rights need to be expanded. What is your opinion? If you were appointed to the U.S. Supreme Court by the President, would you be willing to overturn *Mapp* v. *Ohio* and *Miranda* v. *Arizona*? Why or why not?

THE COURTS

CHAPTER SUMMARY

Chapter 8 describes the history and origins of the American criminal court system. The **state** and **federal court systems** are described, including a discussion of the hierarchy of **trial** and **appellate** courts. An explanation of the importance of the concept of **jurisdiction** is offered.

A history of American courts is provided, including an explanation for the distinction between federal and state courts. The development of state courts is examined, including a discussion of the various levels of courts: (1) **trial courts of limited jurisdiction**, (2) **trial courts of general jurisdiction**, and (3) **appellate courts**.

The Florida court system is used as an example of a state court system that has undergone dramatic changes in an effort to streamline its courts and achieve greater efficiency. One of the recent developments designed to enhance the efficiency of court processing is the increasingly important role of **state court administrators**. Many states, including Florida, have created a statewide office of court administrator. These offices are responsible for a wide range of tasks, including the development of a budget for the courts, the analysis of case flow and backlogs, and the collection and publication of statistics relevant to the state court system.

Recent efforts at the evaluation of courts are examined, with special emphasis on the goals and performance indicators developed by the U.S. Bureau of Justice Statistics. The recent rise in the use of alternatives to criminal courts is discussed, especially through the use of **dispute resolution centers**, sometimes known as neighborhood justice centers.

The federal court system is discussed in detail, with particular emphasis on its origins and growth over the last 200 years. The U.S. Constitutional provisions related to the creation and empowerment of the federal courts are outlined, including the Judiciary Act of 1789, the Judiciary Act of 1925, and the Magistrate's Act of 1968. The federal system currently consists of three levels: (1) **U.S. district courts**, (2) **U.S. courts of appeals**, and (3) the **U.S. Supreme Court**.

The various components of the federal system are described, with an explanation of the concept of **judicial review** and the purpose of the *writ of certiorari*. The cases of *Marbury* v. *Madison* and *Mapp* v. *Ohio* are used as examples of the changing and complex nature of judicial review. Ideas that have been suggested for changing the structure of the federal courts are outlined, including the creation of a National Court of Appeals.

The various components of pretrial court activity are then covered, including the first appearance; bail (and alternative bail programs); the preliminary hearing; the grand jury; and arraignment. The **first appearance** (sometimes called initial appearance) before a magistrate allows for an objective assessment of the legality of the arrest, informs the accused of the charges, and provides an opportunity to set bail. The magistrate's review serves primarily as a method to determine if the arresting officer had probable cause to believe (1) that a crime had been or was being committed, and (2) that the defendant was the person who committed the crime. The first appearance must be made in a timely fashion, a standard which has changed over the years. The 1991 U.S. Supreme Court case of *County of Riverside (California)* v. *McLaughlin* formalized a long-standing rule of thumb by requiring that the first appearance of the accused be made within 48 hours of the arrest.

Bail is the posting of a bond that serves as a pledge to return for future hearings. Some alternative bail programs that have been developed include: **Release on Recognizance (ROR)**; **property bonds**; **deposit bail**; **conditional release**; **third-party custody**; **unsecured bond**; and **signature bond**. **Pretrial release** is a common practice, with as many as 85% of state defendants and 82% of federal defendants being released on some form of bail prior to trial. However, in recent years a movement to reduce the number of defendants out on bail in the interests of public safety has gained momentum. **Danger laws** have been passed in a number of states to restrict the types of crimes for which defendants are eligible for bail.

A **preliminary hearing** is a sort of "mini-trial" that allows the defendant to challenge the legal basis for his or her detention by examining the evidence in the case and attempting to have it disallowed or refuted. The prosecution only needs to present enough evidence to establish to the judge's satisfaction that there is probable cause to believe that a crime has been committed and that the defendant committed it.

Grand jury proceedings are an attempt to provide a check on the prosecutor's discretion, eliminate those cases for which there is insufficient evidence, and investigate possible wrongdoing in the community. Grand juries meet in secret and a person under investigation has no legal right to be present or even notified of a grand jury investigation. If a majority of the members of the grand jury vote to support the charges against the accused, the indictment is given a "true bill" and the prosecution of the accused proceeds.

Arraignment formally informs the defendant of the charges and provides an opportunity for the defendant to enter a **plea**. The defendant can enter one of three pleas: (1) guilty, (2) not guilty, and (3) *nolo contendere* (no contest).

A lengthy discussion of **plea bargaining** and its importance to the smooth operation of the courts is presented. The various facets of plea bargaining, the views of the U.S. Supreme Court on negotiated pleas, the prevalence of guilty pleas, and some of the unintended consequences of plea bargaining are also discussed.

LEARNING TIP

GROUP STUDY

Group study can be very beneficial. However, make sure to select individuals who are attentive in class, those who ask questions, and those who participate and take notes. While it is good to join with people who have similar educational drives, it is also useful to form groups consisting of individuals from diverse backgrounds. The difference in backgrounds may offer a variety of perspectives and better insight to the course material. Lastly, keep the size to less than six people. Large groups are often counterproductive to effective studying.

KEY TERMS

Federal Court System: The three-tiered structure of federal courts, involving U.S. District Courts, U.S. Courts of Appeal, and the U.S. Supreme Court.

State Court Systems: Bodies created to enforce laws passed by state legislatures. State court systems are typically composed of a variety of trial courts, an intermediate appellate court, and a supreme court.

Jurisdiction: The territory, subject matter, or persons over which a court may lawfully exercise its authority.

> Examples: traffic court, family court, juvenile court, each of which deal with special subject matter.

Appellate Jurisdiction: The lawful authority of a court to review a decision made by a lower court.

> Example: Indiana Supreme Court, which has appellate jurisdiction over the Indiana Court of Appeals, but not the Ohio courts.

Judicial Review: The power of a court to review actions and decisions made by other agencies of government.

Trial de novo: A new trial. Applied to cases which are appealed, usually from a court of limited jurisdiction.

> Example: If a defendant receives a traffic ticket and is found guilty by a magistrate, the defendant would have the option of appealing the conviction in traffic court to the court of original jurisdiction, where a trial de novo would be held in the matter. This rarely happens.

Original Jurisdiction: The lawful authority of a court to hear or act upon a case from its beginning and to pass judgment on the law and the facts.

> Example: In some states, the circuit courts have original jurisdiction over any legal matter that occurs within the county, including civil and criminal cases, divorces and other family law matters, and juvenile cases.

Appeal: Generally, the request that a higher court review the decision of a lower court.

> Example: Jones is found guilty of robbery at trial, but feels that the trial judge incorrectly excluded some witnesses that would have established his innocence. Jones appeals the conviction on procedural grounds to the Intermediate Appellate Court.

Court Administrator: Coordinating personnel who assist with case flow management, budgeting of operating funds, and court docket administration.

Circuit Courts: Courts that have general trial jurisdiction over matters not assigned by statute to the county courts and also hear appeals from county court cases.

Pretrial Release: The release of an accused person from custody, for all or part of the time before or during prosecution, upon his or her promise to appear in court when required.

Writ of Certiorari: If an appellate court agrees to review a case, it issues a *writ of certiorari* to a lower court, ordering it to send the records of the case forward for review.

Trial Court: Where serious criminal cases begin. Trial courts conduct arraignments, set bail, take pleas, conduct trials, and impose sentences upon a finding of guilt.

Lower Court: Trial courts of limited or special jurisdiction Lower courts are authorized to hear only less serious criminal cases, usually involving misdemeanors—traffic violations, family disputes, small claims, and so on.

Court of Last Resort: The highest level appellate court in a state system. Used to indicate that no other appellate route remains to a defendant within the state court system once the high court rules on a case.

> Example: In Indiana, the Indiana Supreme Court is the court of last resort.

Plea: In criminal proceedings, a defendant's formal answer in court to the charges against them.

Plea Bargaining: A negotiated agreement between the defendant, prosecutor, and the court as to what an appropriate plea and associated sentence should be.

> Example: Harry Halverson is arrested and charged with 56 counts of mail fraud in a pyramid scheme. Halverson agrees to plead guilty to 5 counts, in exchange for the prosecutor dropping the other 51 counts. Halverson saves the government the expense of a trial (or several trials) and avoids a possible lengthy prison sentence.

Bail Bond: A document guaranteeing the appearance of the defendant in court as required and recording the pledge of money or property to be paid to the court if he or she does not appear.

Release on Recognizance (ROR): The pre-trial release of a criminal defendant on his or her written promise to appear.

Property Bond: The setting of bond in the form of land, houses, stocks, or other tangible property.

Dispute Resolution Centers: Informal hearing infrastructures designed to mediate interpersonal disputes without need for the more formal arrangements of criminal trial courts.

> Example: Fried and Furlow are neighbors who have a long-simmering dispute over a variety of issues, including the Frieds' barking dog and the Furlow's teenage children who play loud rock music. The police are called out one Friday evening. Rather than make an arrest, they refer the neighbors to the local Dispute Resolution Center to see if the differences can be worked out through a trained volunteer mediator.

First / Initial Appearance: An appearance before a magistrate whereby the legality of a defendant's arrest is initially assessed and the defendant is informed of the charges. At this stage bail may be set or pretrial release arranged.

Nolo Contendere: A plea of "no contest." Useful in avoiding an admission of guilt that might be used in subsequent civil suits which might be filed after criminal conviction.

> Example: A truck driver is speeding down the highway and is unable to stop for a red light. He goes through the intersection at approximately 40 m.p.h, striking a vehicle broadside and killing both the occupants. At his criminal trial, he pleads nolo contendere to avoid having his admission of guilt used against him in the subsequent civil action brought by the families of the victims.

KEY CASES

U.S. v. *Montalvo-Murillo* (1990): A defendant has no right to freedom simply because of a "minor" violation of the provisions of the federal Bail Reform Act of 1984.

U.S. v. *Hazzard* (1984): Upheld the federal Bail Reform Act and held that Congress was justified in providing for the denial of bail to offenders who represent a danger to the community.

County of Riverside (CA) v. *McLaughlin* (1991): "A jurisdiction that provides judicial determinations of probable cause within 48 hours of arrest will, as a general matter, comply with the promptness requirement..." Weekends and holidays are not excluded from this 48-hour provision, and in some cases, an even quicker arraignment may be appropriate.

Keeney v. *Tamayo-Reyes* (1992): Defendant is entitled to a federal evidentiary hearing only "if he can show cause for his failure to develop the facts in the state court proceedings and actual prejudice resulting from that failure, or if he can show that a fundamental miscarriage of justice would result from failure to hold such a hearing."

Herrera v. *Collins* (1993): New evidence of innocence is no reason for a federal court to order a new state trial if constitutional grounds are lacking.

Marbury v. *Madison* (1803): Established the U.S. Supreme Court's authority as final interpreter of the U.S. Constitution. Chief Justice John Marshall: "It is emphatically the province of the judicial department to say what the law is..."

Santobello v. *New York* (1971): Plea bargaining is an important and necessary component of the American system of justice.

Henderson v. *Morgan* (1976): Defendant was allowed to withdraw his guilty plea nine years after it was given, because he felt he had not been completely advised as to the nature of the charge or the sentence he might receive as a result of the plea.

PRACTICE TEST QUESTIONS

MULTIPLE CHOICE

8-1. State courts are generally divided into three levels, with _____ at the top of the hierarchy.
   a. courts of last resort
   b. trial courts
   c. courts of limited jurisdiction
   d. intermediate appellate courts
   e. none of the above

8-2. The "jurisdiction" of a court refers to
   a. the geographical area it covers.
   b. the subject matter it deals with.
   c. its place in the hierarchy of the court system.
   d. all of the above
   e. none of the above

8-3. When the U.S. Supreme Court orders the lower court to "forward up the record" of a case that has been tried so the High Court can review it, it issues a
   a. *writ of mandamus.*
   b. *writ of certiorari.*
   c. *writ of trial de novo.*
   d. *nolo contendere.*
   e. true bill.

8-4. The primary traditional purpose of bail was to
   a. deter future offenses.
   b. protect the community from criminals.
   c. examine the sufficiency of the evidence against the accused.
   d. ensure the appearance of the accused individual at trial.
   e. none of the above

8-5. Appeals generally fall into all of the following categories except:
   a. frivolous appeals.
   b. ritualistic appeals.
   c. nonconsensual appeals.
   d. consensual appeals.

8-6. _____ programs release defendants on their own after a promise to appear at court, with no requirement for paying a monetary bail.
   a. Property bond
   b. Signature bond
   c. Preventive detention
   d. Release on recognizance
   e. Cross my heart

8-7. A grand jury has all of the following characteristics and duties except:
   a. may initiate prosecution independent of the prosecutor.
   b. delivers a verdict of guilty or not guilty in criminal trials.
   c. determines if an accused individual should be held over for an actual trial.
   d. meets in secret, with no opportunity for the accused to cross-examine witnesses.

8-8. The plea of *nolo contendere* has its advantages over a guilty plea because it
   a. usually results in a lighter sentence for the offender.
   b. protects the accused in the event of a subsequent civil suit.
   c. limits the judge's sentencing alternatives.
   d. allows the defendant to use a legal loophole to avoid responsibility.
   e. none of the above

8-9. The 1803 case of _____ established the U.S. Supreme Court's authority as final interpreter of the U.S. Constitution.
   a. *Marbury* v. *Madison*
   b. *Herrera* v. *Collins*
   c. *McNabb* v. *U.S.*
   d. *Brady* v. *U.S.*

8-10. The _____ is a sort of "mini-trial" that allows the defendant to challenge the legal basis for his/her detention by examining the evidence in the case and attempting to have it disallowed or refuted.
   a. grand jury
   b. arraignment
   c. preliminary hearing
   d. first appearance
   e. none of the above

TRUE–FALSE

_____ 8-11. Grand juries meet in secret and a person under investigation has no legal right to be present or even notified of a grand jury investigation.

_____ 8-12. Federal judges are usually elected officials who then serve "life" terms on the bench.

_____ 8-13. The case of *Marbury* v. *Madison*, decided in 1803, was the first instance in which the U.S. Supreme Court declared its authority to review the actions of Congress that it found to conflict with the Constitution.

_____ 8-14. In the 1993 case of *Herrera* v. *Collins*, the U.S. Supreme Court ruled that new evidence of innocence is not a sufficient reason for a federal court to order a new state trial if there are no constitutional grounds for appeal.

_____ 8-15. The federal court system consists of three tiers, including the U.S. District Courts, U.S. Courts of Appeal, and the U.S. Supreme Court.

_____ 8-16. The jurisdiction of a court can refer to the territory, subject matter, or persons over which a court may lawfully exercise its authority.

_____ 8-17. Dispute resolution centers are generally not allowed to mediate disputes when criminal charges are pending against either of the disputants.

_____ 8-18. The U.S. Supreme Court has ruled that plea bargaining is an important and necessary component of the American system of justice.

_____ 8-19. The U.S. Supreme Court has ruled that new evidence proving the innocence of a defendant is not sufficient reason for a federal court to order a state court to grant a new trial.

_____ 8-20. The courts have generally upheld the notion that suspects cannot be detained indefinitely and that defendants must be brought before a magistrate for a first appearance within 48 hours of arrest.

MATCHING

a. first appearance	g. circuit courts
b. *nolo contendere*	h. judicial review
c. *trial de novo*	i. *writ of certiorari*
d. court of last resort	j. preliminary hearing
e. court administrator	k. release on recognizance
f. bail bond	l. arraignment

_____ 8-21. Courts of general jurisdiction that may hear matters not assigned by statute to the county courts.

_____ 8-22. This is issued when an appellate court agrees to hear a case, to order the lower court to forward up the records of the case.

_____ 8-23. The pre-trial release of a defendant based on a written promise to appear at future hearings.

_____ 8-24. Literally, a new trial.

_____ 8-25. The highest level of appellate court in a state system.

_____ 8-26. An appearance before a magistrate where the legality of the defendant's arrest is reviewed and the defendant is informed of the charges.

_____ 8-27. A plea of no contest.

_____ 8-28. Court employee who assists with the management of cases, budgeting, and docket administration.

_____ 8-29. The power of a court to review actions and decisions made by other agencies of government, such as the legislative or executive branches.

_____ 8-30. A sort of "mini-trial" where the defendant has the opportunity to challenge the legal basis for his/her detention by examining the evidence in the case and attempting to refute it.

DISCUSSION EXERCISES

Judges and Bail Decisions

Bail or No Bail?

1. Salvadore Lopez, is a 52-year-old farm worker who cannot read. He has a wife and two children. Lopez was charged with smuggling guns, marijuana, and other narcotics across the Mexican border. The prosecutor, when discussing the case with the news media, says that he suspects Mr. Lopez of being a person who has been transporting guns and drugs for years, but who, until now, has avoided being arrested by authorities. Mr. Lopez claims that he is completely innocent and wouldn't know what marijuana looked like if he saw it. Should he be detained or released? How much bail would you set in order to release? What other information would you need to know?

2. Roger A. Kearney, is a 27-year-old electrical engineer. He is charged with vehicular homicide stemming from the death of Chris Pariano. Pariano was stepping out of his pickup truck when Kearney sped down the wrong side of the street. Kearney was drunk at the time, police said. The police also learned that he had eight previous convictions for drunk driving and 19 other serious vehicular offenses. Should he be detained or released? How much bail would you set in order to release? What other information would you need to know?

3. Edward Savitz is a 50-year-old single man who has a good-paying full-time job and lives in an expensive high-rise apartment. He is charged with the statutory rape of a 16-year-old, sexual abuse of two others, and corrupting the morals of a minor. It is alleged that he paid to have sex with hundreds of boys, but on all occasions, the young men agreed to participate. The maximum sentence that he can receive for his crimes is 5 to 10 years. Mr. Savitz has been diagnosed as having the AIDS virus. Should he be detained or released? How much bail would you set in order to release? What other information would you need to know?

4. Frank Anderson was, at the age of 19, convicted of rape and sentenced to prison for 3 years. Approximately 1 year after his release, he became a suspect in a number of robberies of older men. He threatened a number of the victims with bodily harm if they filed complaints. One 71-year-old victim nevertheless agreed to cooperate with the authorities, and Anderson was arrested and charged for robbery. Shortly after his first initial appearance, he was released on bail. Anderson then broke into the 71-year-old man's house, beat him, kicked him numerous times, and stole $3,000 and a gun. The victim suffered a concussion and needed seven stitches. Anderson was identified and again apprehended, and was charged with an additional count of robbery. Again, he was released on bail for $1,500. Anderson returned to the home of the victim, assaulted him, and attempted to stop him from cooperating with the police. He was once again apprehended and this time charged with aggravated battery. Should he be detained or released? How much bail would you set in order to release? What other factors would you want to know?

5. An 18-year-old girl, Kim Walak, was arrested for shoplifting. She claimed to be indigent (poor), with no steady source of income. She lived with an unemployed boyfriend, and she dropped out of school in the 11th grade. She had one prior arrest for shoplifting, but those charges were dismissed for unknown reasons. Should she be detained or released? How much bail would you set in order to release? What other factors would you need to know?

THE COURTROOM WORK GROUP AND THE CRIMINAL TRIAL

CHAPTER SUMMARY

Chapter 9 examines the main participants in the criminal trial process, primarily concentrating on the **judge**, the **prosecutor**, and the **defense attorney**. The trial process is then outlined in detail. The concept of a **courtroom work group** is based on the notion that two groups of participants are involved in the trial process—"professionals" (such as the judge, the prosecutor, and the defense attorney) and "outsiders" (such as the defendant, the victim, and the jurors).

The judge is responsible for administering the courtroom and ensuring that all cases are tried in an objective manner. The judge holds ultimate authority in the courtroom, determines whether evidence will be admitted or excluded, sometimes determines guilt or innocence (in the absence of a jury), and usually determines the sentence after an offender has been convicted.

Judges are selected through a popular election, an appointment from a politician, or a combination of appointment and election (the so-called **Missouri Plan**). The qualifications to be a judge range from a law degree (for courts of general jurisdiction and appellate courts) to no requirements (for some courts of limited jurisdiction, such as traffic court). The power of judges is usually balanced by a statewide **judicial conduct commission**, and judges who abuse their power can be censured or impeached, although this is quite rare.

The local prosecuting attorney is usually an elected official who serves a four-year term of office. Federal U.S. Attorneys are appointed by the U.S. Attorney General. In most cities, the prosecuting attorney hires a number of assistants who handle the majority of cases. Prosecutors have a tremendous amount of **discretion** in deciding which cases to try and what charges should be filed in the case. Prosecutors may also advise the local police on legal matters and help guide criminal investigations. If a prosecutor abuses his/her discretionary power, charges can be filed with the state, but this is extremely rare. Usually the only recourse available would be to vote the prosecutor out of office in the next election.

The defense attorney is charged with being an advocate for the defendant, and this involves a wide variety of activities, from investigating the state's evidence to filing motions to entering into plea negotiations. There are three basic types of defense counsel: **private attorneys**, **court-appointed counsel**, and **public defenders**. Since the 1963 case of *Gideon* v. *Wainwright*, attorneys have been appointed for felony defendants who cannot afford one (indigent defendants). Three systems are used to provide these attorneys: court-assigned counsel, public defenders, and contract arrangements. Most public defenders are tremendously overworked and unable to provide the resources necessary to match the case presented by the prosecution.

A variety of other professional participants are involved in the criminal trial process. The **bailiff** is the court officer responsible for maintaining order in the courtroom and supervising the jury when it is sequestered. **Local court administrators** make sure the courts function efficiently, manage the budget, and help with the jury. The **court recorder** creates and maintains a transcript of all that occurs during a trial. The **clerk of the court** maintains court records, issues summonses and subpoenas, and performs other administrative tasks. **Expert witnesses** are called upon to provide their special knowledge on matters of relevance to a particular case. They are allowed to express their opinion or draw conclusions based on their particular field of knowledge.

Nonprofessional participants are also critical to the trial process. **Lay witnesses** are individuals who have information that is relevant to a particular case (such as an eyewitness to a crime), who are not considered experts. They can only testify as to what they saw, heard, etc., and are not allowed to express an opinion or draw conclusions. **Jurors** are picked through a variety of means, such as voter registration rolls, and are supposed to represent a cross-section of the community. The **victim** has become almost a forgotten participant in some courtrooms. Since the prosecutor is actually representing the state, the victim can play little or no role in the actual handling of the case. In some cases the victim may not be aware of a plea bargain that has taken place or that a case has come to trial. Likewise, the **defendant's** role is ill-defined in the current trial process. The defendant may choose to take an active role in his/her own defense, or may simply allow the defense attorney to make all of the important decisions related to the case.

The trial itself is held to determine the guilt or innocence of the accused, which can be done by a **jury** or a judge (in the case of a bench trial). Our system is **adversarial** in nature, which means that the trial is a type of contest, with both sides striving to win within the limits of the law. A trial must be held in a timely manner and must be open to the public. The jury is selected through a process called *voir dire* (to speak the truth). Potential jurors can be removed through **challenges for cause, peremptory challenges,** or a **challenge to the array.** After a jury is selected, each side makes an opening statement. Then the prosecution presents its case. **Evidence** is presented through the use of **testimony** and can be either **direct** or **circumstantial** in nature. **Hearsay** evidence is generally not admissible in court, although exceptions (such as a dying declaration) are made. The defense challenges the case presented by the prosecution and attempts to cast doubt on the reliability or accuracy of the witnesses. **Closing arguments** by both sides summarize the important points and attempt to persuade the jury to emphasize certain facets and ignore others. The judge then provides instructions to the jury, the jury deliberates, and returns a verdict. In cases of conviction, the judge is then responsible for determining an appropriate **sentence**.

LEARNING TIPS

"CRAMMING" FOR EXAMS

Obviously, "cramming" (trying to learn a tremendous amount in a short period) is not a desirable strategy, but if cramming is inevitable, follow these guidelines: Because you do not have time to learn everything, make a plan of attack. Instead of jumping into everything, decide what is most likely to be on the exam and concentrate on those items. Decide what is the most important material and recite it over and over. This method helps ingrain the material in your mind. And lastly, do not criticize yourself. It is hard to learn when you are constantly reminding yourself what you should have done.

NOTE-TAKING

Pay special attention to key words. Names, equations, vocabulary, quotations, and words of degree are examples of key words. Focusing on key words will eliminate excess material from cluttering your notes. More importantly, key words are wonderful review mechanisms because they recall images and lectures, and serve to connect similar images.

KEY TERMS

Judge: An elected or appointed public official who presides over a court of law and who is authorized to hear and sometimes to decide cases, and to conduct trials.

Prosecutor: An elected or appointed public official, licensed to practice law, whose job it is to conduct criminal proceedings on behalf of the state or the people against an accused person.

Prosecutorial Discretion: The decision-making power of prosecutors based upon the wide range of choices available to them in the handling of criminal defendants.

Defense Counsel: A licensed trial lawyer, hired or appointed to conduct the legal defense of an individual accused of a crime and to represent him or her before a court of law.

Public Defender: An attorney employed by a government agency for the purpose of providing defense services to indigents.

Adversarial System: The two-sided structure under which American criminal trial courts operate and which pits the prosecution against the defense.

Bailiff: The court officer whose duties are to keep order in the courtroom and to maintain physical custody of the jury.

Expert Witness: A person who has special knowledge recognized by the court as relevant to the determination of guilt or innocence.

Juror: A member of a jury, selected for jury duty, and required to serve as an arbiter of the facts in a court of law. Jurors are expected to render verdicts of guilt or innocence as to the charges brought against an accused, although they may sometimes fail to do so (as in the case of a hung jury).

Subpoena: A written order issued by a judicial officer, prosecutor, defense attorney, or grand jury, requiring a specific person to appear in a designated court at a specified time in order to testify in a case under the jurisdiction of that court or to bring material to be used as evidence to that court.

Change of Venue: The movement of a suit or trial from one jurisdiction to another, or from one location to another within the same jurisdiction. A change of venue may be made in a criminal case to assure a defendant a fair trial.

> Example: Stephen Stevenson is accused of murdering the daughter of Jonestown's mayor. Stevenson's defense attorney requests that a change of venue to Smithville (in a neighboring county) be granted so that pre-trial publicity and community outrage aren't as much of a factor at the trial.

Speedy Trial Act: A 1974 federal law requiring that proceedings in a criminal case against a defendant begin before passage of a specified period of time, such as 70 working days after indictment. Some states also have speedy trial requirements.

Lay Witness: An eyewitness, character witness, or any other person called upon to testify who is not considered an expert.

Peremptory Challenge: A means of removing unwanted potential jurors without the need to show cause for their removal.

> Example: Because her client was accused of raping a sixteen-year-old girl, the defense attorney used one of her peremptory challenges to remove a potential juror who was the mother of three teenage daughters.

Challenge for Cause: A means of removing potential jurors from consideration due to their inability to be fair or impartial in deciding a particular case.

> Example: The wife of a police officer might be challenged for cause by the defense in a case involving a police officer who has been shot.

Sequestered Jury: One which is isolated from the public during the course of a trial and throughout the deliberation process.

Opening Statement: The initial statement of an attorney made in a court of law to a judge and/or jury, describing the facts that he or she intends to present during trial in order to prove his or her case.

Evidence: Anything useful to a judge or jury in deciding the facts of a case.

Direct Evidence: Evidence which, if believed, directly proves a fact.

> Example: The surveillance video from a convenience store showing the robbery taking place would be considered direct evidence.

Circumstantial Evidence: Evidence which requires interpretation or which requires a judge or jury to reach a conclusion based upon what the evidence indicates.

> Example: Fred Fleener testifies that he saw the defendant, Andy Arnold, enter the victim's house. Then Fleener heard a shot and saw Arnold run quickly from the house with a gun in his hand. Fleener did not see the crime occur, and the judge or jury must draw its own inferences concerning the actions of the defendant.

Real Evidence: Consists of physical material or traces of physical activity.

> Example: A murder weapon would be considered real evidence.

Testimony: Oral evidence offered by a sworn witness on the witness stand during a criminal trial.

Perjury: The intentional making of a false statement as part of testimony by a sworn witness in a judicial proceeding on a matter material to the inquiry.

Hearsay: Something which is not based upon the personal knowledge of a witness.

The Hearsay Rule: The long standing American courtroom precedent that hearsay cannot be used in court. ... the American trial process asks that the person who was the original source of the hearsay information be brought into court to be questioned and cross-examined.

> Example: Rocko is on trial for murder. His wife's best friend, Rosie, calls the prosecutor and wants to testify that Rocko's wife had confided to her that Rocko had bragged about committing the murder. The prosecutor explains to Rosie that this testimony is inadmissible since the original source of the information (Rocko's wife) would have to be the one to testify concerning the conversation.

Closing Argument: An oral summation of a case presented to a judge, or to a judge and jury, by the prosecution or by the defense in a criminal trial.

> Comment: Defense attorney Johnnie Cochran's now-famous "If it doesn't fit, you must acquit" speech took place during closing arguments in the O.J. Simpson trial.

Verdict: In criminal case processing, a formal and final finding made on the charges by a jury and reported to the court, or by a trial judge when no jury is used.

Courtroom Work Group: Professional courtroom actors, including judges, prosecuting attorneys, defense attorneys, public defenders, and others who earn a living serving the court.

KEY CASES

Edmonson v. *Leesville Concrete Co., Inc.* (1991): Peremptory challenges based on race are not acceptable in civil lawsuits.

Michigan v. *Lucas* (1991): The Sixth Amendment guarantee of the right to confront witnesses does not necessarily extend to evidence of a prior sexual relationship between a rape victim and a criminal defendant, and thus rape shield statutes are acceptable.

Powers v. *Ohio* (1991): The prosecution cannot systematically exclude jurors on the basis of race through the use of peremptory challenges.

Burns v. *Reed* (1991): "A state prosecuting attorney is absolutely immune from liability for damages ... for participating in a probable case hearing, but not for giving legal advice to the police."

Demarest v. *Manspeaker* (1991): Federal prisoners who are subpoenaed to testify are entitled to witness fees just as nonincarcerated witnesses would be.

Imbler v. *Pachtman* (1976): "State prosecutors are absolutely immune from liability ... for their conduct in initiating a prosecution and in presenting the state's case."

Mu'Min v. *Virginia* (1991): Being aware of a case through pretrial publicity alone is not enough to disqualify a juror. If a juror can be shown to be unbiased by the publicity, they can still serve.

Maryland v. *Craig* (1990): Closed-circuit television can be used to shield children who testify in criminal courts.

White v. *Illinois* (1992): In-court testimony given by a medical provider and the child's babysitter, which repeated what the child had said to them concerning the defendant's sexually abusive behavior, was not subject to hearsay restrictions and was permissible.

Crosby v. *U.S.* (1993): A defendant may not be tried in absentia even if he/she was present at the beginning of a trial where his/her absence is due to escape or failure to appear.

Zafiro v. *U.S.* (1993): Defendants charged in federal courts with similar or related offenses may be tried together, even when their defenses differ substantially.

Fex v. *Michigan* (1993): "common-sense compels the conclusion that the 180-day period (speedy trial provision) does not commence until the prisoner's disposition request has actually been delivered to the court and prosecutor of the jurisdiction that lodged the detainer against him."

Doggett v. *U.S.* (1992): A delay of 8-1/2 years violated the speedy trial provisions because it resulted from government negligence.

Georgia v. *McCollum* (1992): Defendants (and their attorneys) cannot use peremptory challenges to exclude potential jurors on the basis of race.

Brady v. *Maryland* (1963): The prosecution is required to disclose to the defense exculpatory evidence that directly relates to claims of either guilt or innocence.

U.S. v. *Bagley* (1985): The prosecution must disclose any evidence that the defense requests.

Powell v. *Alabama* (1932): The Fourteenth Amendment required state courts to appoint counsel for defendants in capital cases who were unable to afford their own attorney.

Johnson v. *Zerbst* (1938): Indigent defendants have a right to receive the assistance of appointed counsel in all criminal proceedings in federal court.

Gideon v. *Wainwright* (1963): Extended the right to appointed counsel in state courts to all indigent defendants charged with a felony.

Argersinger v. *Hamlin* (1972): The U.S. Supreme Court required that adequate legal representation be given to any defendant facing a potential sentence of imprisonment.

In re Gault (1967): Extended right to appointed counsel to juveniles.

Nix v. *Whiteside* (1986): A lawyer's duty to a client "is limited to legitimate, lawful conduct compatible with the very nature of a trial as a search for truth ... counsel is precluded from taking steps or in any way assisting the client in presenting false evidence or otherwise violating the law."

Thiel v. *Southern Pacific Company* (1945): It is not necessary for every jury to contain representatives of every conceivable racial, ethnic, religious, gender, and economic group in a community, but court officials may not systematically and intentionally exclude any juror solely because of his or her social characteristics.

Klopfer v. *North Carolina* (1967): The right to a speedy trial in federal and state court is a fundamental guarantee of the U.S. Constitution.

Baker v. *Wingo* (1972): Sixth Amendment guarantees to a speedy trial could be illegally violated even in cases where the accused did not explicitly object to delays.

Strunk v. *United States* (1973): Denial of a speedy trial should result in a dismissal of all charges against the accused.

Witherspoon v. *Illinois* (1968): A juror opposed to the death penalty could be excluded from a jury if it were shown that (1) the juror would automatically vote against conviction without regard to the evidence, or (2) the juror's philosophical orientation would prevent an objective consideration of the evidence.

Batson v. *Kentucky* (1986): The use of peremptory challenges for apparently purposeful discrimination constitutes a violation of the defendant's right to an impartial jury.

Griffin v. *California* (1965): If a defendant refuses to testify, prosecutors and judges are prohibited from even commenting on the fact, other than to instruct the jury that such a failure to testify cannot be held to indicate guilt.

PRACTICE TEST QUESTIONS

MULTIPLE CHOICE

9-1. The Missouri Plan is a mechanism suggested by the American Bar Association for
    a. limiting judicial discretion during sentencing.
    b. the merit plan selection of judges.
    c. reducing endless appeals by defendants
    d. speeding the flow of cases through the courts.
    e. none of the above

9-2. As discussed in the text, criminal law is a field that
   a. few law students actively choose to pursue.
   b. has high financial rewards for most practitioners.
   c. attracts many prestigious lawyers.
   d. is a high status segment of the legal profession.
   e. all of the above

9-3. *Gideon* v. *Wainwright*, decided in 1963 by the U.S. Supreme Court, held that
   a. in federal cases, the right to counsel becomes applicable as soon as a defendant is arrested.
   b. the right to counsel applies not only to state defendants charged with felonies, but in all trials of defendants that might result in a jail sentence.
   c. a defendant has a right to counsel when submitting a guilty plea to the court for any offense.
   d. the right to appointed counsel applies to all indigent defendants in state court who are charged with a felony.
   e. all of the above

9-4. Indigency refers to criteria used by
   a. the state police in establishing crime enforcement levels.
   b. the local prosecutor's office to determine how vigorously to pursue a defendant in a criminal case.
   c. the courts to establish the amount of bail.
   d. judges to determine eligibility of defendants for court-appointed counsel.

9-5. Under the _____ system, legal services for defendants are provided by individual private practice attorneys who are selected and paid for by the court from a roster of all practicing criminal attorneys within the jurisdiction of the trial court.
   a. public defender
   b. court appointed counsel
   c. retained counsel
   d. contract

9-6. As discussed in your text, the motion for discovery is a request by the defense attorney to
   a. obtain detailed information about the charges.
   b. move the trial to a different part of the jurisdiction.
   c. suppress certain evidence that was illegally seized.
   d. examine all of the evidence that will be presented at trial.

9-7. Changing the "venue" of a trial
   a. removes the prosecutor due to a conflict of interest.
   b. removes the judge due to a conflict of interest.
   c. removes the defendant due to a conflict of interest.
   d. moves the trial to another location due to pretrial publicity.

9-8. An impartial jury, in constitutional terms, means one that
   a. comes only from voter registration rolls.
   b. is generally representative of the population.
   c. has no prior knowledge, of any kind, of the offender or the offense.
   d. has no restrictions against persons in any age, sex, race, religious, or occupational category.
   e. all of the above

9-9. In jury selection, challenges for cause
   a. are only made by the defense.
   b. are not required to be justified by the attorney requesting the challenge.
   c. deal with sound legal reasons for removing potential jurors.
   d. are ruled upon by the prosecuting attorney.
   e. all of the above

9-10. The murder weapon would primarily be considered to be _____ evidence.
    a. direct
    b. real
    c. testimonial
    d. damning

TRUE–FALSE

_____ 9-11. The process by which a jury is interviewed by the prosecutor and defense counsel is called *voir dire*.

_____ 9-12. When utilizing a challenge for cause, a juror can be excused by either the defense or prosecution and no reason for doing so needs to be stated.

_____ 9-13. A witness states that although she didn't see the defendant commit the crime, she did see the defendant arguing with and threatening the victim shortly before the crime occurred. This would be an example of circumstantial evidence.

_____ 9-14. According to the U.S. Supreme Court, the prosecution must disclose any evidence related to a case that the defense requests.

_____ 9-15. The phrase courtroom work group refers to all persons who are licensed to practice law and who earn their living primarily in the courtroom.

_____ 9-16. A motion for a bill of particulars asks the court to order the prosecution to provide detailed information about the charges which the defendant will be facing in court.

_____ 9-17. A challenge to the array indicates that the defense attorney does not believe that the pool from which the jury is being selected is representative of the community at large.

_____ 9-18. If a defense attorney is aware that his client is about to commit perjury on the stand, he is obligated to inform the court of this fact, even if it violates the attorney-client privilege.

_____ 9-19. If a defendant chooses not to testify at his/her trial, the prosecutor is allowed to comment on this and point out to the jury that an innocent person would want to take the stand in an effort to clear his/her name.

_____ 9-20. Hearsay evidence, or evidence that is not based upon the personal knowledge of the witness, is automatically excluded from the courtroom, regardless of the circumstances.

MATCHING

a. Judge
b. circumstantial evidence
c. subpoena
d. direct evidence
e. change of venue
f. hearsay
g. bailiff
h. perjury
i. expert witness
j. real evidence
k. peremptory challenge
l. challenge for cause

_____ 9-21. Evidence that consists of physical material or traces of physical activity, such as tire tracks.

_____ 9-22. Removing an unwanted potential juror without the need to disclose a reason for their removal.

_____ 9-23. Evidence which requires interpretation or which requires the judge or jury to reach a conclusion based upon the evidence presented.

_____ 9-24. A person who has special knowledge recognized by the court as relevant to the determination of the guilt or innocence of the accused.

_____ 9-25. A statement that is not based upon the personal knowledge of a witness.

_____ 9-26. A false statement made by a sworn witness during a judicial proceeding.

_____ 9-27. Moving a trial from one jurisdiction to another.

_____ 9-28. Court officer who keeps order in the courtroom and maintains custody of the jury.

_____ 9-29. A written order requiring someone to appear in court to testify.

_____ 9-30. An elected or appointed public official who presides over a court of law.

DISCUSSION EXERCISES

Ethical Issues for the Courtroom Workgroup: Put yourself in the place of each of the courtroom workgroup participants listed below and try to decide how you would deal with these dilemmas.

The Prosecutor

1. While preparing the case against an accused homicide defendant, you discover a witness who provides an alibi for the defendant. Do you tell the defense attorney about your discovery? Would it make any difference if the defendant were involved in organized crime? Drug dealing?

2. After you have successfully prosecuted a rapist, you uncover evidence which indicates that the victim in the case made the whole story up to avenge a love affair that went sour. What do you do?

3. While preparing the case against an accused drug dealer, you discover that the primary witness for the defense is wanted for more serious crimes in another state. Should you seek to have the witness extradited immediately or wait until after the trial?

4. While investigating a child molestation case, you interview the teenage victim who expresses a fear of talking to the defense attorney and the defense investigators. Should you advise the victim not to talk to the defense if she doesn't feel comfortable doing so?

The Defense Attorney

1. You receive a phone call from a person who, along with two buddies, has been charged with distribution of marijuana. He wants you to represent all three of them. The other two suspects have no money, and your contact offers to pay the legal fees for all three of them (up front, in cash). Should you represent all three codefendants jointly?

2. You are asked to represent a defendant who cannot afford to pay your full fee at the present time. Should you work out an arrangement so that your client pays you a $1,000 retainer now and pays the rest of the fee if and when she is acquitted (recognizing that conviction would result in incarceration and no real opportunity to earn the money for your fee)?

3. During your client's sentencing for child molesting, the prosecutor informs the judge that your client has no previous record. Your client has revealed to you in confidence several similar prior convictions in other jurisdictions. Should you disclose this fact to the judge?

4. Your client informs you that she did in fact murder her mom. Should you inform the court of this information? Possessing such knowledge, should you allow your client to take the stand and deny her guilt?

The Judge

1. At arraignment, you ask a defendant if he has yet obtained counsel. He replies that he wants to defend himself. He has a fifth-grade education and works as a day laborer for a local construction firm. He is charged with armed robbery and faces ten years in prison. Should you let him defend himself?

2. You are assigned to preside over a jury trial in a gruesome homicide case that has been widely publicized in the area. Although the defense does not request it, should you order a change of venue?

3. You are asked to decide a sexual molestation case. Your daughter was molested by a neighbor 10 years earlier. Should you decide this case? Should you inform both sides of this information? What if you are the only judge in the district?

4. You are a death penalty advocate assigned to sentence a capital case. Should you decide the sentence in this case? What if you are an anti-death penalty advocate? Should you decide the case?

Jurors

1. You have been summoned for jury duty. During *voir dire* for a capital murder case, the prosecutor questions your attitude toward the death penalty. You are strongly in favor of the death penalty. Should you sit on this trial? (If the prosecutor has used all of her peremptory challenges, should you be excluded for cause?)

2. You are 21 years old and have been called to serve jury duty. Although you consider yourself to be a good candidate for jury duty, you are not from this area, since you are attending the local university. Your name was on the voter registration polls since you registered to vote in the presidential election last year. This county allows students to be excused from jury duty without comment merely because of their status. Should you take advantage of this technicality to avoid jury duty?

3. You are called for jury duty and during the course of the trial you notice two of the other jurors sitting together and talking in animated language during every break. You suspect that these jurors are discussing the merits of the case, in direct violation of the judge's instructions to wait until all of the evidence is in before entering into deliberations. Should you tell the bailiff? The judge? Anyone?

SENTENCING

CHAPTER SUMMARY

Chapter 10 begins with a discussion of the philosophy of criminal sentencing and outlines the major rationales or goals we use for punishing offenders: retribution, incapacitation, deterrence (general and specific), rehabilitation, and restoration. The advantages and disadvantages of each are detailed.

Two types of sentencing based on these punishment goals are called indeterminate and determinate. Problems with the indeterminate model led to the rise of determinate sentencing, which is more prevalent today. Indeterminate sentencing relies on a rehabilitative philosophy and is prone to greater sentencing disparity, since the judge and the parole board are responsible for determining how long an offender's sentence should be. The determinate model attempts to curb judicial discretion but doesn't take into account individual differences in offenders and the circumstances surrounding a crime.

In 1984, Federal Sentencing Guidelines were established to reduce sentencing confusion, eliminate sentencing disparities, and permit flexibility in introducing aggravating and mitigating factors that might impact on a particular crime. These guidelines provide for sentencing ranges for specific types of crimes, and judges must follow the guidelines or risk appellate review. The federal sentencing guidelines have created many problems in the federal courts and prisons, and will have a greater impact in the years to come.

The presentence investigation (PSI) report is an optional tool used in most state and federal jurisdictions that allows the judge to have more information in making a sentencing decision. The creation of the PSI is usually the responsibility of the probation department and includes information about the offender's personal and criminal history, the offender's attitude toward the offense and their participation in it, and (in some cases) a sentencing recommendation from the probation officer who completed the report. Little verification of the information provided by the defendant is accomplished.

Victim impact statements are an attempt to allow the victim of a crime to have some input into the sentencing decision. The statement allows the victim to inform the judge of the losses (physical, emotional, financial) he or she has suffered as a result of the actions of the offender. The courts have sent mixed messages on the weight that should be given to victim impact statements, but most judges see them as an important component in arriving at an appropriate punishment for the offender.

Four traditional sanctions continue to dominate the thinking of most legislators and judges: incarceration (in a jail or prison), probation, fines, and death. Most felony offenders receive some sort of incarceration as part of their sentence: most misdemeanor offenders are sentenced to probation. More and more jurisdictions are also utilizing monetary sanctions in addition to incarceration or probation to further punish the offender and increase the revenues available to the justice system.

Capital punishment has received more and more attention in the last ten years, but it is still an infrequent and erratic sanction. There is both opposition and support for the death penalty. Opponents argue that the death penalty is: (1) irreversible if an error is made and the wrong person is executed, (2) not an effective deterrent, (3) arbitrary and discriminatory, and (4) reduces the state to the same moral level as the offender. Proponents of the death penalty rely on three basic arguments: (1) revenge, (2) just deserts, and (3) protection. Public support for the death penalty comes and goes, but it is becoming more and more apparent that even though most people support the death penalty in abstract terms, most are also reluctant to apply it in specific instances.

LEARNING TIPS

ANSWERING QUESTIONS ON EXAMS

Answer the shortest, simplest questions first. This will give you increased confidence for the more difficult questions to follow. In other words, answer the matching, true/false, fill-in or multiple choice questions. End with essay and short-answer questions. If you get stuck on a question, look for associations or answers in the other test questions. Most importantly, budget and monitor your time. Do not spend half of your time on questions which are worth only twenty percent of the exam. If you are completely stuck, move on.

MULTIPLE CHOICE

Multiple choice questions can be very confusing. First, check to see how many answers you are supposed to choose for each question. Second, read and answer the questions without looking at the test answers. If your answer matches one of the test answers, choose it. This will avoid additional confusion by the other test answers. Third, if you don't know the answer exactly, read each choice because answers are often quite similar. Fourth, any questions which you are not able to answer immediately should be skipped until you have time to return to them.

KEY TERMS

Sentencing: The imposition of a criminal sanction by a judicial authority.

Retribution: The act of taking revenge upon a criminal perpetrator.

Incapacitation: The use of imprisonment or other means to reduce the likelihood that any offender will be capable of committing future offenses.

Deterrence: A goal of criminal sentencing which seeks to prevent others from committing crimes similar to the one for which an offender is being sentenced.

Specific Deterrence: A goal of criminal sentencing which seeks to prevent a particular offender from engaging in repeat criminality.

Example: The "three strikes" statues that mandate a life sentence for offenders convicted of three separate felonies are said to be designed to prevent an offender from perpetually victimizing communities.

General Deterrence: A goal of criminal sentencing which seeks to prevent others from committing crimes similar to the one for which a particular offender is being sentenced by making an example of the person sentenced.

> Example: A mayor decides to reduce the amount of prostitution in the city by publishing the names of the customers (sometimes called "Johns") of the prostitutes in the local paper.

Rehabilitation: The attempt to reform a criminal offender. Also, the state in which a reformed offender is said to be.

Restoration: A goal of criminal sentencing which attempts to make the victim "whole again."

> Example: Sal Benedict was convicted of reckless driving for sideswiping a car driven by 75-year-old Seymour Green. As part of the sentence, Benedict was required to take meals to Mr. Green's house while he recuperated and volunteer 2,000 hours of community service at Mr. Green's favorite charities.

Indeterminate Sentencing: A model of criminal punishment which encourages rehabilitation via the use of general and relatively unspecific sentences.

> Example: New York State gives offenders a sentence such as 5-to-15 years, and the New York State parole board is charged with determining when the offender is ready for release from prison.

Good Time: The amount of time deducted from time to be served in prison on a given sentence... contingent upon good behavior and / or awarded automatically by application of a statute or regulation.

> Example: Indiana credits an offender with one day of "good time for" every day served, so a ten-year sentence would result in five years of imprisonment.

Determinate Sentencing: A model for criminal punishment which sets one particular punishment, or length of sentence, for each specific type of crime.

Aggravating Circumstances: Those elements of an offense or of an offender's background which could result in a harsher sentence under the determinate model than would otherwise be called for by sentencing guidelines.

> Example: John Jones was identified as the leader of a gang of youths who robbed a local convenience store owner. Jones was the only one with a gun, which he used to pistol whip the store owner.

Mitigating Circumstances: Those elements of an offense or of an offender's background which could result in a lesser sentence under the determinate model than would otherwise be called for by sentencing guidelines.

> Example: Using the previous example, Jimmy Juniper was a 14-year-old acquaintance of John Jones. Jones threatened to beat Juniper if he didn't go along on the robbery. Juniper had no criminal record, and when the youths were apprehended, Juniper made a full confession and agreed to testify against Jones as well as make restitution to the store owner.

Presentence Investigation: The examination of a convicted offender's background prior to sentencing.

Victim Impact Statement: The in-court use of victim- or survivor-supplied information by sentencing authorities wishing to make an informed sentencing decision.

Capital Punishment: Another term for the death penalty.

Capital Offense: A criminal offense punishable by death.

Just Deserts: As a model of criminal sentencing, one which holds that criminal offenders deserve the punishment they receive at the hands of the law and that punishments should be appropriate to the type and severity of the crime committed.

Truth in Sentencing: A close correspondence between the sentence imposed upon those sent to prison and the time actually served prior to prison release.

KEY CASES

Wilkerson v. *Utah* (1878): Upheld the use of the firing squad as a method of execution.

Coker v. *Georgia* (1977): The U.S. Supreme Court concluded that the death penalty was not an acceptable punishment for the crime of rape, concluding that execution would be "grossly disproportionate" to the crime.

Payne v. *Tennessee* (1991): Reversed the *Booth* decision made four years earlier and held that "victim impact evidence is simply another form or method of informing the sentencing authority about the specific harm caused by the crime in question, evidence of a general type long considered by sentencing authorities."

Furman v. *Georgia* (1972): "Evolving standards of decency" might necessitate a reconsideration of the constitutionality of capital punishment. Allowing the jury to decide guilt and the punishment of death at the same time allowed for an arbitrary and capricious application of the death penalty.

Woodson v. *North Carolina* (1976): Laws requiring the mandatory application of the death penalty for specific crimes are prohibited.

Coleman v. *Thompson* (1991): State prisoners condemned to die cannot cite "procedural default" (such as a defense attorney's failure to meet a filing deadline for appeals in state court) as the sole reason for an appeal to federal court.

Mistretta v. *U.S.* (1989): Congress acted appropriately in the creation of the federal sentencing guidelines, and the guidelines could be applied in federal cases nationwide.

Gregg v. *Georgia* (1976): The two-step process of a judge or jury deciding guilt and then undertaking a separate sentencing phase was specifically upheld by the U.S. Supreme Court.

McCleskey v. *Zandt* (1991): Limited the number of appeals available to a condemned person. After the first appeal, the defendant must show (1) why the subsequent appeal wasn't included in the first appeal and (2) how the defendant was harmed by the absence of the claim.

In re Kemmler (1890): "Punishments are cruel when they involve torture or a lingering death; but the punishment of death is not cruel, within the meaning of that word as used in the Constitution."

Booth v. *Maryland*: (1987) Using victim impact statements in a capital case violated the Eighth Amendment ban on cruel and unusual punishment and could result in the death penalty being imposed in an arbitrary and capricious manner.

Smith v. *U.S.* (1993): A defendant who trades firearms for drugs "uses" the firearms within the meaning of federal sentencing guidelines and may be sentenced to a harsher prison term as a result.

Deal v. *U.S.* (1993): It is possible to try and convict a defendant for six separate offenses in a single proceeding and use the federal sentencing guidelines to convict and sentence the defendant as a career offender as a consequence.

PRACTICE TEST QUESTIONS

MULTIPLE CHOICE

10-1. Modern sentencing practices are influenced by which of the following five goals?
   a. retribution
   b. incapacitation
   c. deterrence
   d. rehabilitation
   e. all of the above

10-2. This philosophy of sentencing seeks to prevent others from committing crimes similar to the one for which an offender is being sentenced.
   a. rehabilitation
   b. retribution
   c. deterrence
   d. incapacitation

10-3. The rehabilitative approach to sentencing eventually became known as the _____ of corrections.
   a. just deserts model
   b. medical model
   c. restoration model
   d. psychological healing model

10-4. _____ sentencing relies heavily upon a judge's discretion to choose among types of sanctions and set upper and lower limits on the length of prison stays.
   a. Intermediate
   b. Indeterminate
   c. Determinate
   d. Deterrent

10-5. Which official is responsible for conducting presentence investigations in most jurisdictions?
   a. prosecutor
   b. probation/parole officer
   c. judge
   d. defense attorney

10-6. Much of the philosophical basis of today's victims' movement can be found in the _____ model.
   a. restorative justice
   b. retribution
   c. restitution
   d. none of the above

10-7. A 1994 study of efficacy of victim impact statements found that judicial sentencing decisions were _____ affected by them.
   a. greatly
   b. rarely
   c. modestly
   d. never

10-8. Which of the following is not one of the retentionist justifications for the death penalty?
    a. deterrence
    b. revenge
    c. just deserts
    d. protection

10-9. The future of the death penalty rests primarily with:
    a. the president.
    b. state legislatures.
    c. congress.
    d. all of the above

10-10. This U.S. Supreme Court case created the two-step trial procedure which separated the determination of guilt and sentencing stages.
    a. *Gregg* v *Georgia.*
    b. *Poyner* v *Murray.*
    c. *Furman* v *Georgia.*
    d. *Simpson* v. *Darden*
    e. None of the above.

TRUE–FALSE

_____ 10-11. Sentencing philosophies are manifestly intertwined with issues of religion, morals, values, and emotions.

_____ 10-12. The overall goal of deterrence is crime prevention.

_____ 10-13. Consecutive sentences are served at the same time.

_____ 10-14. Determinate sentencing is also sometimes called presumptive, or fixed, sentencing.

_____ 10-15. Mitigating circumstances result in harsher sentences under the determinate model.

_____ 10-16. Truth in sentencing means that probation officers have presented their presentence investigation report based on the truths they uncovered.

_____ 10-17. Myers and Talarico's 1987 study of sentencing practices in Georgia found an abundance of system-wide bias and discrimination.

_____ 10-18. Most judges deny the presentence report writer's recommendations.

_____ 10-19. Between 1967 and 1977, a de facto moratorium existed with no executions carried out in any U.S. jurisdiction.

_____ 10-20. Justifications for the death penalty are collectively referred to as the retentionist position.

MATCHING

a. retribution
b. incapacitation
c. specific deterrence
d. rehabilitation
e. indeterminate sentencing
f. good time

g. determinate sentencing
h. aggravating circumstances
i. mitigating circumstances
j. presentence investigation
k. capital offense
l. truth in sentencing

_____ 10-21. The examination of a convicted offender's background prior to sentencing.

_____ 10-22. A goal of criminal sentencing which attempts to prevent a particular offender from engaging in repeat criminal behavior.

_____ 10-23. An attempt to have a close correspondence between the sentence imposed and the actual time served.

_____ 10-24. The attempt to reform a criminal offender.

_____ 10-25. A sentence of 2–12 years would be an example of this.

_____ 10-26. The amount of time deducted from time to be served in prison on a given sentence based upon good behavior while in prison.

_____ 10-27. The act of taking revenge upon a criminal perpetrator.

_____ 10-28. A model for criminal punishment which sets one particular punishment, or length of sentence, for each specific type of crime.

_____ 10-29. Factors surrounding an offense which could result in a harsher sentence under the determinate model.

_____ 10-30. A criminal offense punishable by death.

DISCUSSION EXERCISES

Judges and Sentencing Decisions I

If you were a judge, what sentence would you give each of the following defendants? What factors would be most important to you?

1. Mr. White is 24 years old and was one of 18 active draft protesters convicted of refusing to register for the draft. Some of the convicted protesters have been put on probation, and four others have been incarcerated for nearly three years. Mr. White's brother and uncle were killed in Vietnam, and he claims that his refusal to register was a political statement regarding the war.

2. Miss Colby, a 32-year-old single mother, was convicted of reckless driving. On January 23, she was driving while intoxicated along State Street, and hit a parked fire truck. The fire department was responding to an emergency medical call, attempting to transport an elderly man suffering a heart attack to the hospital. Because of the accident, the man could not be transported until another transport vehicle arrived. Miss Colby was originally charged with Driving While Intoxicated, but the prosecutor allowed her to plead to reckless driving.

3. Daniel Driver, 35 years old, was convicted on felony child molestation charges. He was on parole for similar charges at the time of the current offense. Mr. Driver is divorced, works as a computer consultant for an electronics firm, and has been described as an "active churchgoer."

4. Maria Campo, 40, pled guilty to two counts of passing bad checks. Ms. Campo had been purchasing new furniture for her apartment, paying with checks for which she had no funds. She has two previous convictions for forgery.

5. Thomas "Ziggy" Petruzzelli, 16, was convicted on involuntary manslaughter charges. The fight that led to the stabbing happened on July 4 outside a convenience store. Ziggy was standing outside the store asking adults to buy him a pack of cigarettes – something he could not do as a minor. Bruce Deuce, 33, agreed to buy the cigarettes, but when Deuce came back outside the store, the two began arguing. Ultimately, Ziggy's father got involved, intervening with a two-by-four. His father is currently awaiting trial on an assault with a deadly weapon charge.

Sentencing Decisions II

1. Darryl Jackson is a 20-year-old unemployed black male. He is addicted to cocaine, has no family, and is homeless. He has three prior felony convictions for drug possessions. He has recently been convicted of his fourth felony (a burglary), and you are the judge deciding his fate. The sentencing statute allows you to sentence Darryl to anything from a minor fine to life imprisonment (or any combination of punishments).

   The specific facts of the case:

   On October 18, Darryl Jackson entered the apartment of Angela Strater. He entered by picking the lock on her back door. He stole her stereo ($1,500), jewelry ($3,500), and matchbox car collection ($800). Upon leaving her apartment, Darryl was apprehended by a security officer for the Strater burglary. Darryl claimed he needed to sell the goods so that he would have money for food. What sentence would you give Darryl?

2. Ron Kuzak is a 20-year-old white male. He is a college student with a 3.6 grade point average, works part-time at McDonald's, and goes to church on Sunday (he sings in the choir). He is also addicted to cocaine. He has three prior felony convictions for drug possessions. He has recently been convicted of his fourth felony (a burglary), and you are the judge deciding his fate. The sentencing statute allows you to sentence Ron to anything from a minor fine to life imprisonment (or any combination of punishments).

   The specific facts of the case:

   On October 18, Ron Kuzak entered the apartment of Angela Strater. He entered by picking the lock on her back door. He stole her stereo ($1,500), jewelry ($3,500), and matchbox car collection ($800). Upon leaving her apartment, Ron was apprehended by a security officer for the Strater burglary. Ron claimed he needed to sell the goods so that he would have money for college tuition. What sentence would you give Ron?

C H A P T E R

PROBATION, PAROLE, AND COMMUNITY CORRECTIONS

CHAPTER SUMMARY

Chapter 11 examines that subset of the correctional realm known as community corrections, with particular emphasis on probation and parole. The philosophy behind both probation and parole is similar—that an offender can be rehabilitated or reformed more effectively in a community setting than in an incarcerative one.

A brief history of both probation and parole is offered, as well as a definition for each concept. The conditions that are commonly imposed on probationers and parolees are defined, and some statistical background is provided as to the size of the offender population that is typically sentenced to serve their time under some form of community supervision.

The advantages and disadvantages of probation and parole are discussed at length. Advantages of probation and parole include: (1) lower cost; (2) increased employment opportunities; (3) greater likelihood of restitution for victims; (4) maintenance of a community support network for the offender; (5) reduced risk of criminal socialization; (6) increased use of community services; and (7) increased opportunity for rehabilitation. Disadvantages of probation and parole include (1) relative lack of punishment; (2) increased risk to the community; (3) increased social costs.

The legal environment of probation and parole is the next topic, and the major U.S. Supreme Court cases related to the topic are discussed. Major cases include: *Mempa* v. *Rhay* (1967), *Morrissey* v. *Brewer* (1972, *Gagnon* v. *Scarpelli* (1973), *Greenholtz* v. *Nebraska* (1979), and *Bearden* v. *Georgia* (1983). All of these cases address the question of how much freedom and responsibility a person sentenced to probation or parole should be allowed and what due process rights should be granted to offenders on probation or parole.

The federal probation system is briefly discussed, and an outline presents the Job of a Probation/Parole Officer, emphasizing the duties and responsibilities involved. Two models common to community corrections officers—the social work and the correctional—are examined.

The chapter then turns to a discussion of the move toward innovative options in sentencing. It touches upon such recent concepts as split sentencing, shock probation/parole, shock incarceration, mixed sentencing, community service, intensive supervision, and home confinement

The chapter ends with a discussion of the future of probation and parole and the author's prediction that although probation will always be with us in some form, parole may become a victim of the move toward determinate sentencing.

LEARNING TIPS

OPEN-BOOK/OPEN-NOTE EXAMS

While the opportunity to take either an open-book or open-note test may seem extremely lucky, these exams are often the most difficult. Significant preparation may be even more imperative with these exams. To eliminate excess time spent flipping through pages of notes or chapters of a book, prepare thoroughly by using tabs to mark pages, highlighting key words, including an outline in your notes, and knowing the progression of the notes or chapters backwards and forwards.

SHORT ANSWERS

Short-answer questions usually ask for a definition or description and the significance of the question relative to the coursework. Problems arise when students go off on tangents writing everything they know on the topic. It is important to stay focused on the question, be brief and answer the question directly, using facts and key words.

KEY TERMS

Probation: The conditional freedom granted by a judicial officer to an adjudicated adult or juvenile offender, as long as the person meets certain conditions of behavior.

Parole: The status of an offender conditionally released from a prison by discretion of a paroling authority prior to the expiration of sentence, required to observe conditions of parole, and placed under the supervision of a parole agency.

Conditions of Probation and Parole: The general (state ordered) and specific (court- or board-ordered) limits imposed on an offender who is released on either probation or parole.

> Example: As conditions of his probation, Fred Farkas was required to maintain employment, have a permanent address, report any changes in status in employment or living arrangements, and ask permission from his probation officer to take trips outside of the county.

Parole Board: A state paroling authority. Most states have parole boards which decide when an incarcerated offender is ready for conditional release and which may also function as revocation hearing panels.

Caseload: The number of probation and parole clients assigned to one probation or parole officer for supervision.

Probation (or Parole) Violation: An act or a failure to act by a probationer (or parolee) which does not conform to the conditions of probation (or parole).

Probation (or Parole) Revocation: The administrative action of a probation (or paroling) authority removing a person from probationary (or parole) status in response to a violation of lawfully required conditions of probation (or parole), including the prohibition against commission of a new offense and usually resulting in a return to prison.

> Example: Fred Farkas (example above) lost his job and didn't tell his probation officer. The loss of employment led to Fred losing his apartment and, eventually, to his selling

drugs to raise some money. Fred's probation officer moved to revoke his probation based on the (three) above violations of probation.

Restitution: A court requirement that an alleged or convicted offender pay money or provide services to the victim of the crime or provide services to the community.

> Example: Susan Susudio was convicted of drunk driving after running a red light and striking another vehicle. As part of her sentence, Susan was required to pay the medical expenses of the victim of her accident, the deductible on the victim's car insurance, and also perform 500 hours of volunteer work in the emergency room of the local hospital.

Intermediate Sanctions: The use of split sentencing, shock probation and parole, home confinement, shock incarceration, and community service in lieu of other, more traditional, sanctions such as imprisonment and fines.

Split Sentence: A sentence explicitly requiring the convicted person to serve a period of confinement in a local, state, or federal facility followed by a period of probation.

> Example: Horace Silver was sentenced to six months in jail followed by three years on probation.

Shock Probation: The practice of sentencing offenders to prison, allowing them to apply for probationary release and enacting such release in surprise fashion.

Shock Incarceration: A sentencing option which makes use of "boot camp"–type prisons in order to impress upon convicted offenders the realities of prison life.

Mixed Sentence: One which requires that a convicted offender serve weekends (or other specified periods of time) in a confinement facility (usually a jail), while undergoing probation supervision in the community.

> Example: Dave Seville, a barber, was over a year behind in his child support payments. Judge Hardy decided to sentence barber Seville to 30 days in jail, but allowed him to serve his time on his days off. This allowed Seville to keep his job and earn some money to be used in paying off his child support debt.

Community Service: A sentencing alternative which required offenders to spend at least part of their time working for a community agency.

Home Confinement: House arrest. Individuals ordered confined in their homes are sometimes electronically monitored to be sure they do not leave during the hours of confinement (absence from the home during working hours is often permitted).

Intensive Supervision: A form of probation supervision involving frequent face-to-face contacts between the probationary client and probation officers.

Judgment Suspending Sentence: A court-ordered sentencing alternative which results in the convicted offender being placed on probation.

> Example: Roxie Rivers was sentenced to three years in prison. However, the judge suspended the sentence and placed Roxie on probation for three years. If Roxie violates the terms of her probation by committing another offense, she could be ordered to serve the original three-year sentence as well as any additional sentence handed down for the new offense.

KEY CASES

Morrissey v. *Brewer* (1972): The following procedural safeguards are required in revocation hearings involving parolees: (1) written notice of alleged violations; (2) evidence of the violation must be disclosed; (3) a neutral and detached body must constitute the hearing authority; (4) the parolee should have the chance to appear and offer a defense, including testimony, documents, and witnesses; (5) the parolee has the right to cross-examine witnesses; and (6) a written statement should be provided to the parolee at the conclusion of the hearing that includes the body's decision, the testimony considered, and reasons for revoking parole if such occurs.

Gagnon v. *Scarpelli* (1973): Extended the due process rights granted to parolees in *Morrissey* (see above) to probationers and also required that two hearings be held before probation can be revoked—a preliminary hearing and a final hearing. Also provided some indigence relief to probationers facing revocation hearings.

Bearden v. *Georgia* (1983): Probation cannot be revoked for failure to pay a fine and make restitution if it cannot be shown that the defendant was responsible for the failure. Alternative forms of punishment must be considered and be shown to be inadequate before the defendant can be incarcerated.

Greenholtz v. *Nebraska* (1979): Parole boards do not have to specify the evidence used in deciding to deny parole.

Kelly v. *Robinson* (1986): A restitution order cannot be vacated through a filing of bankruptcy.

Minnesota v. *Murphy* (1984): A probationer's incriminating statements to a probation officer may be used as evidence if the probationer did not specifically claim a right against self-incrimination.

Mempa v. *Rhay* (1967): Both notice and a hearing are required in order to revoke probation.

Griffin v. *Wisconsin* (1987): Probation officers may conduct searches of a probationer's residence without need for either a search warrant or probable cause.

Escoe v. *Zerbst* (1935): Probation "comes as an act of grace to one convicted of a crime…" and the revocation of probation without hearing or notice to the probationer was acceptable.

PRACTICE TEST QUESTIONS

MULTIPLE CHOICE

11-1. The man known as the first probation officer, a Boston shoemaker, was
    a. Thomas Mott Osborne.
    b. John Augustus.
    c. John Howard.
    d. Ben Franklin.

11-2. In the 1973 case of *Gagnon* v. *Scarpelli,* the U.S. Supreme Court
    a. stressed the rehabilitative nature of probation.
    b. ruled against the use of hearsay evidence in probation revocation hearings.
    c. affirmed the privilege against self-incrimination revocation hearings.
    d. extended the holding in Morrissey v. Brewer to include probationers.
    e. none of the above

11-3. In most jurisdictions the decision to initially grant parole to an offender is made by
    a. the parole officers.
    b. county parole boards.
    c. state or federal parole boards.
    d. the sentencing court.
    e. none of the above

11-4. Probation and parole
   a. are essentially the same and are terms that are used interchangeably.
   b. use different supervision techniques but are usually administered by the same office.
   c. are sentences handed down by the courts.
   d. are distinctly different forms of community correction administered by different authorities.

11-5. Court decisions have affirmed the correctness of such conditions of probation as
   a. that the probationer must not drink alcoholic beverages.
   b. that the probationer must make restitution to the victim.
   c. that the probationer must attend a drug treatment program.
   d. all of the above
   e. none of the above

11-6. In the event of a technical violation of probation, the _____ would be responsible for initiating violation proceedings.
   a. police
   b. probation officer
   c. judge
   d. prosecutor
   e. none of the above

11-7. _____ is the term discussed in the text which allows for a three- to six-month regimen of military drill, drug treatment, exercise, and academic work in return for having several years removed from an inmate's sentence.
   a. "Good time" law
   b. Shock incarceration
   c. Intensive parole
   d. Intensive probation
   e. none of the above

11-8. All of the following are considered to be advantages of probation and parole except:
   a. lower cost.
   b. increased employment opportunities.
   c. relative lack of punishment.
   d. reduced risk of criminal socialization.
   e. greater likelihood of restitution for victims.

11-9. In the 1967 case of _____, the U.S. Supreme Court determined that both notice of the charges and a hearing are required in order to revoke an offender's probation.
   a. *Gagnon* v. *Scarpelli*
   b. *Morrissey* v. *Brewer*
   c. *Mempa* v. *Rhay*
   d. *Griffin* v. *Wisconsin*

11-10. In the 1983 case of *Bearden* v. *Georgia*, the U.S. Supreme Court determined that
   a. a restitution order cannot be vacated through a filing of bankruptcy.
   b. probation cannot be revoked for failure to pay a fine and make restitution if it can be shown that the defendant was not responsible for the failure.
   c. a probationer's incriminating statements made to a probation officer may be used as evidence against him or her.
   d. probation "comes as an act of grace to one convicted of a crime".

TRUE–FALSE

_____ 11-11. Community service is a sentencing alternative that requires offenders to spend at least part of their time working for a community agency.

_____ 11-12. A split sentence requires an offender to serve at least part of their sentence in a jail or prison, followed by a longer period on probation.

_____ 11-13. When utilizing shock probation, the judge sentences an offender to a prison term, then suspends the sentence before the offender actually starts to serve the sentence in a jail or prison.

_____ 11-14. Restitution is a court requirement that an offender pay money or provide services to the victim of the crime or provide services to the community.

_____ 11-15. Probation is the conditional freedom granted by a judicial officer to an adjudicated adult or juvenile offender after a period of incarceration.

_____ 11-16. Parole is the status of an offender conditionally released from a prison by a paroling authority prior to the expiration of sentence.

_____ 11-17. Few states still have parole boards which decide when an incarcerated offender is ready for conditional release—most of that function has been taken over by prison authorities.

_____ 11-18. The number of probation and parole clients assigned to one probation or parole officer for supervision is referred to as the caseload of the officer.

_____ 11-19. Any act or failure to act by a probationer (or parolee) which does not conform to the conditions of probation (or parole) is referred to as a violation.

_____ 11-20. If a judge orders that a convicted offender's sentence be suspended and places the offender on probation, no further steps can be taken to reinstate the suspended prison time regardless of the offender's behavior while on probation.

MATCHING

a. mixed sentence
b. intensive supervision
c. split sentence
d. shock incarceration
e. shock probation
f. suspended sentence

g. community service
h. intermediate sanctions
i. revocation hearing
j. home confinement
k. special conditions
l. general conditions

_____ 11-21. State-ordered limits imposed on an offender who is released on either probation or parole.

_____ 11-22. Utilized to decide if an offender has violated the terms of his/her probation or parole by committing a new offense or failing to live up to the conditions of probation or parole.

_____ 11-23. Split sentencing, shock probation and parole, home confinement, shock incarceration, and community service are all examples of this.

_____ 11-24. A sentence which explicitly requires an offender to serve a period of confinement in a local, state, or federal facility followed by a period of probation.

_____ 11-25. The practice of sentencing offenders to prison, allowing them to apply for probationary release, and enacting such release in a surprise fashion.

_____ 11-26. "Boot camp"-type prisons used in order to impress upon convicted offenders the realities of prison life.

_____ 11-27. A sentence which requires that a convicted offender serve weekends in jail while on probation supervision in the community during the week.

_____ 11-28. A sentencing alternative which requires offenders to spend at least part of their time working for a community agency.

_____ 11-29. Sometimes called house arrest.

_____ 11-30. A form of probation supervision involving frequent face-to-face contacts between the probationary client and probation officers.

DISCUSSION EXERCISES

On Probation and Parole—To Revoke or Not To Revoke

Let's catch up on the case studies we examined in Chapter 10, on sentencing. All of the case studies listed have been updated to include the sentence received and a brief description of how the offender has performed while out on probation or parole. Your task as the probation/parole officer assigned to the case is to decide whether or not to initiate revocation proceedings against the offender and provide a brief explanation of why you would or would not take this course of action.

1. Mr. White is 24 years old and was one of 18 active draft protesters convicted of refusing to register for the draft. Some of the convicted protesters have been put on probation, and four others have been incarcerated for nearly three years. Mr. White's brother and uncle were killed in Vietnam, and he claimed that his refusal to register was a political statement regarding the war. Mr. White was sentenced to five years on probation, but he hasn't kept his probation officer informed of his employment status or a recent job change.

2. Miss Colby, a 32-year-old single mother, was convicted of reckless driving. On January 23, she was driving while intoxicated along State Street and hit a parked fire truck. The fire department was responding to an emergency medical call, attempting to transport an elderly man suffering a heart attack to the hospital. Because of the accident, the man could not be transported until another transport vehicle arrived. Miss Colby was originally charged with Driving While Intoxicated, but the prosecutor allowed her to plead to reckless driving. She was sentenced to four years on probation and ordered to attend Alcoholics Anonymous meetings on a regular basis. She has not been attending her meetings and was recently picked up for public intoxication when she staggered out of a bar and fell into the street, nearly being struck by a passing police car.

3. Daniel Driver, 35 years old, was convicted on felony child molestation charges. He was on parole for similar charges at the time of the current offense. Mr. Driver is divorced, works as a computer consultant for an electronics firm, and has been described as an "active churchgoer." Mr. Driver was sentenced to five years in prison, but the judge suspended three years of the time with the condition that Driver attend regular therapy sessions with an approved counselor. After serving his prison sentence, Mr. Driver has been attending therapy sessions, but failed to register with the state's new "Sex Criminal Registry." He has also been spotted by police officers hanging around the park on weekends.

4. Maria Campo, 40, pled guilty to two counts of passing bad checks. Ms. Campo had been purchasing new furniture for her apartment, paying with checks for which she had no funds. She has two previous convictions for forgery. The judge sentenced her to two years; with good time she was released after serving 11 months in the county jail. Ms. Campo was seen with a known felon coming out of a liquor store. Upon further investigation, you learn that she wrote a check to purchase beer in the store.

5. Thomas "Ziggy" Petruzzelli, 16, was convicted on involuntary manslaughter charges. The fight that led to the stabbing happened on July 4 outside a convenience store. Ziggy was standing outside the store asking adults to buy him a pack of cigarettes—something he could not do as a minor. Bruce Deuce, 33, agreed to buy the cigarettes, but when Deuce came back outside the store, the two began arguing. Ultimately, Ziggy's father got involved, intervening with a two-by-four. His father was convicted on an assault with a deadly weapon charge and sent to state prison. Ziggy got probation, but has been unco-

operative, failing to report for scheduled meetings, refusing to seek employment, and missing his nightly curfew on several occasions. On a recent home visit, Ziggy's probation officer spotted a handgun on the night stand next to Ziggy's bed.

What do you think of chain gang proposals? What might be some of the unintended consequences of this type of activity? Will exposing how prisons operate to greater public scrutiny lead to any potential problems for prison administrators? Should the type of crime committed or the characteristics of the offender have any bearing on who works on the chain gang?

Prisoners Should Work—But Not Busting Rocks

That was some visual they hooked up in Alabama last week, where inmates were shown in chains, breaking rock. Alabama, which reintroduced chain gangs last spring, is about as tough on inmates as they come. Too bad it's all so worthless.

Prison shouldn't be a breeze, obviously. And it makes sense to put prisoners to work. The public spends billions yearly to imprison 1 million plus inmates. But rather than make convicts sweat for the purpose, why not make them work for their keep? Why not give them the means to pay victim restitution? Why not keep them occupied and out of trouble?

It can be done. In 1993, North Carolina paid 1,800 inmates $1 to $3 an hour for work in prison industries ranging from paint manufacturing to motor oil repackaging. The work generated almost $1 million for the state's general fund.

In 1989, Oregon hired private-sector supervisors to create a blue jean company with prison labor. By 1994, Prison Blues were on sale in 17 states and five countries.

Almost every state runs a few prison industries, and hard-core Alabama, where inmates do everything from making license plates to inputting data, is no exception.

States are careful not to take jobs from citizens, which is why some restrict the sale of inmate products and others seek enterprises for which there is no local labor.

But this is not what chain gangs are about. They are political creations designed to exploit the twin misperceptions that: a) prisoners have it easy; and b) hard time deters new crime.

Anyone who has visited a medium-security prison knows life there isn't easy. And despite 20 years of research, studies fail to show any link between severity of punishment and recidivism. Yet chain gangs are catching fire. Arizona has started a similar program. Florida is about to begin one, and Kansas

and Wisconsin lawmakers are thinking about it.

That's all just wasted energy. Gang labor is likely to harden prisoners against the system, not teach them to work with it. Moreover, it's just dumb to use chains along highways. Imagine what would happen if a truck hit a gang of five prisoners.

Recently, one gang inmate was unable to work after suffering an epileptic seizure. He was returned to the prison and chained to a bar outside for the rest of the day.

That tells the truth about chain gangs. They aren't meant to deter crime or make inmates productive. They are meant to humiliate, to be cruel and vindictive. That's not profitable, and it's surely not progress.

Reprinted with permission of USA Today.

PRISONS AND JAILS

CHAPTER SUMMARY

Chapter 12 examines the history of corrections in the United States, outlining some of the corporal punishments such as flogging, mutilation, and branding that were popular during the Colonial era. Public humiliation, workhouses, and the concept of transportation are also discussed.

The Quakers in Pennsylvania were instrumental in suggesting what they considered to be the more humanitarian alternative of the incarceration, resulting in the Penitentiary Era (1790-1825). The Mass Prison Stage (1825-1876) was initiated with the opening of Auburn Prison in New York, and this proved to be a popular variation on the original Quaker concept. The Reformatory Stage (1876-1890) was a short-lived period marked by the contributions of Captain Alexander Maconochie of Norfolk Island fame (the mark system) and Sir Walter Crofton's Irish Prison System, with its so-called ticket of leave. The Elmira Reformatory in New York State, under the leadership of Zebulon Brockway, incorporated the early release concepts pioneered by Maconochie and Crofton.

The Industrial Prison Era (1890-1935) developed a number of approaches to the effective use of inmate labor, including the contract system, the piece-price system, the lease system, the public account system, the state use system, and public works. Some of these practices are still in use today. The Punitive Era (1935-1945) de-emphasized the importance of inmate labor and emphasized the importance of custody in the prison environment. As rehabilitation became more popular, the Era of Treatment (1945-1967) experienced a resurgence. Most treatment was based on a Medical Model, which held that offenders were "sick" and could be "cured" through the use of the most appropriate treatment. The Community-Based Format (1967-1980) was the logical extension of this philosophy, and an increase in the use of smaller, more treatment oriented facilities was common. During the Reagan/Bush years, Warehousing (1980-1995) of offenders was prevalent, while a renewed emphasis on punishment characterizes the current Just Deserts Era (1995-present).

Various methods of calculating the number of inmates a correctional facility can hold are discussed, including rate capacity, operational capacity, and design capacity. The cost of building and maintaining a prison is also detailed. A brief overview of the statistical characteristics of prisons today is provided.

A discussion of the issues surrounding jails is undertaken, with special attention to women in jail, crowding in jails, and direct supervision jails, as well as some predictions concerning jails and the future. The increased use of private prisons is outlined, as well as an examination of the various security levels found in most correctional systems.

Finally, the federal prison system is discussed, and some recent improvements such as accreditation and training, are mentioned.

LEARNING TIPS

ESSAY QUESTIONS ON EXAMS

Essay questions cause anxiety for many students. To reduce anxiety, read the entire question first. Then re-read the question, underlining key words and noting specific parts and instructions within the question. Third, write a quick outline. This will keep your answer focused, as well as minimize your chances of forgetting important parts. Finally, due to the grading of essay exams being partly subjective, it is good practice to write legibly, skip lines, keep your answer concise, and utilize only one side of the paper.

STUDY GROUPS

A variety of purposes can be accomplished with study groups. Reviewing previous class lectures could help answer any question or uncertainties in your notes. Groups can practice teaching one another, providing unique insight to the material. Closer to test time, study groups are a great source for compiling potential test questions. Also, general discussions within the group are a great way to learn the material and to reinforce your memory.

KEY TERMS

Prison: A state or federal confinement facility having custodial authority over adults sentenced to confinement.

Lex Talionis: The law of retaliation. Under *lex talionis* the convicted offender was sentenced to a punishment which most closely approximated the original injury.

Workhouse (Brideswell): A form of early imprisonment whose purpose was to instill habits of industry in the idle.

Pennsylvania Style (penitentiary): A form of imprisonment developed by the Pennsylvania Quakers around 1790 as an alternative to corporal punishment. The style made use of solitary confinement and resulted in the nation's first penitentiary.

Auburn System (also Congregate but Silent System): A form of imprisonment developed in New York State around 1820 which depended upon mass prisons, where prisoners were held in congregate fashion. This style of imprisonment was a primary competitor with the Pennsylvania style.

Reformatory Concept: A late-nineteenth-century correctional model based upon the use of the indeterminate sentence and belief in the possibility of rehabilitation of offenders, especially for youthful offenders.

Industrial Prisons: Those which flourished during the industrial prison era and whose intent it was to capitalize on the labor of convicts sentence to confinement.

Ashurst-Sumners Act: 1935 federal legislation which effectively ended the industrial prison era by restricting interstate commerce in prison-made goods.

State-Use System: A form of inmate labor in which items produced by inmates are salable only by or to state offices.

> Examples: license plates, hunting licenses, picnic tables for state parks, etc.

ADMAX: Administrative maximum; the term used by the federal government to denote ultra-high security prisons.

The Medical Model: A theoretical framework for the handling of prisoners which held that offenders were "sick" and could be "cured" through the application of behavioral and other appropriate forms of therapy.

Community Corrections: A sentencing style which represents a movement away from traditional confinement options and an increased dependence upon correctional resources which are available in the community.

Work-release: A prison program in which inmates are temporarily released into the community in order to meet job responsibilities.

Warehousing: An imprisonment strategy based upon the desire to prevent recurrent crime but which has abandoned any hope of rehabilitation.

Recidivism: The repetition of criminal behavior.

Nothing Works Doctrine: The belief that correctional treatment programs had little success in rehabilitating offenders.

Prison Capacity: A general term referring to the size of the correctional population an institution can effectively hold. There are three types of prison capacity: design, rated, and operational.

Design Capacity: The number of inmates a prison was architecturally intended to hold when it was built or modified.

Rated Capacity: The size of the inmate population a facility can handle according to the judgment of experts.

Operational Capacity: The number of inmates a prison can effectively accommodate based upon management considerations.

Justice Model: A contemporary model of imprisonment in which the principle of just deserts forms the underlying social philosophy.

Jail: A confinement facility administered by an agency of local government, typically a law enforcement agency, intended for adults but sometimes also containing juveniles, which holds persons detained pending adjudication and/or persons committed after adjudication, usually those committed on sentences of a year or less.

Direct Supervision Jail: Temporary confinement facilities which eliminate many of the traditional barriers between inmates and correctional staff.

Private Prisons: Correctional institutions operated by private firms on behalf of state and local governments.

Privatization: The movement toward the wider use of private prisons.

PRACTICE TEST QUESTIONS

MULTIPLE CHOICE

12-1. The group which most influenced the beginnings of the American prison experience was (were) the
a. Pilgrims.
b. Quakers.
c. Catholic Church.
d. Salvation Army.
e. none of the above

12-2. The first American penitentiary, opened in the late 1700s in Philadelphia, was called
a. Alcatraz.
b. Huntsville prison.
c. Walnut Street jail.
d. Eastern penetentury.
e. none of the above

12-3. One of the first attempts at parole, as practiced by Sir Walter Crofton in Ireland, allowed offenders to earn a conditional release by meeting certain objectives. Release was granted under a
a. mark system.
b. ticket of leave.
c. good behavior rule.
d. marx system.
e. short release.

12-4. The feature of the Eastern and Western penitentiaries that most clearly characterized the Pennsylvania correctional philosophy of the nineteenth century was
a. congregate cell blocks.
b. the whipping post.
c. corporal punishment.
d. solitary confinement.
e. all of the above

12-5. Auburn Prison, established in 1823 in New York State, attempted to reform prisoners by
a. enforcing the "codes of confinement."
b. torturing them.
c. forced labor and use of the silent system.
d. use of the pleasure-pain principle.

12-6. During the early decades of this century, there was opposition to prison industries primarily because they
a. exploited inmate labor.
b. threatened the jobs of workers in the free world.
c. were counterproductive to rehabilitative ideals.
d. were threats to prison security.
e. none of the above

12-7. The 1981 U.S. Supreme Court case of *Rhodes* v. *Chapman* dealt with the issue of prison overcrowding and held that
a. placing two inmates in a cell is cruel and unusual punishment.
b. placing two inmates in a cell is not cruel and unusual punishment.
c. inmates must show that prison officials exhibited "deliberate indifference" by not dealing with the overcrowding issue at an earlier date.

    d. inmates have a reasonable expectation of privacy that is violated by having to share their cell with another inmate.

    e. none of the above

12-8. _____ house the most serious offenders and are characterized by double and triple security patterns.

    a. Maximum-security prisons

    b. Reformatories

    c. Medium-security prisons

    d. Minimum-security prisons

    e. none of the above

12-9. The term used by the federal government to denote ultra-high security prisons is

    a. ADMAX.

    b. MAXIMAX.

    c. ULTRAMAX.

    d. SUPERMAX.

    e. HYPERMAX.

12-10. The number of inmates a prison was architecturally intended to hold when it was built or modified is called

    a. prison capacity.

    b. rated capacity.

    c. operational capacity.

    d. design capacity.

TRUE–FALSE

_____ 12-11. An overview of the various approaches to correctional treatment suggests that programs that focus on offender rehabilitation should be abolished completely.

_____ 12-12. Most deaths that occur in jails are the result of natural causes.

_____ 12-13. A state or federal confinement facility having custodial authority over adults sentenced to confinement for less than one year is called a prison.

_____ 12-14. Under lex talionis the convicted offender was sentenced to a punishment which most closely approximated the original injury.

_____ 12-15. The Pennsylvania System, also called the Congregate but Silent System, was a form of imprisonment developed in 1820 which depended upon mass prisons, where prisoners were held in congregate fashion.

_____ 12-16. Prisons which flourished during the Industrial Prison Era, and whose intent it was to capitalize on the labor of convicts sentenced to confinement, were part of the Reformatory Concept.

_____ 12-17. The 1935 federal legislation which effectively ended the industrial prison era by restricting interstate commerce in prison-made goods was called the Taft-Hartley Act.

_____ 12-18. Direct supervision jails are temporary confinement facilities which eliminate many of the traditional barriers between inmates and correctional staff.

_____ 12-19. The movement toward the wider use of private prisons is called corporationalization.

_____ 12-20. A late-nineteenth-century correctional model based upon the use of the indeterminate sentence and belief in the possibility of rehabilitation of offenders especially for youthful offenders was called the Progressive Model.

MATCHING

a. workhouse (brideswell)
b. Pennsylvania System
c. Auburn System
d. Reformatory Concept
e. state-use system
f. Medical Model

g. community corrections
h. work release
i. warehousing
j. recidivism
k. Nothing Works Doctrine
l. Justice Model

_____ 12-21. The repetition of criminal behavior.

_____ 12-22. A form of early imprisonment designed to instill a work ethic in the idle.

_____ 12-23. A form of imprisonment developed by the Quakers which made use of solitary confinement and resulted in the nation's first penitentiary.

_____ 12-24. A contemporary model of imprisonment in which the principle of just deserts forms the underlying social philosophy.

_____ 12-25. A form of inmate labor in which items produced by inmates are salable only to state agencies.

_____ 12-26. A belief that offenders are "sick" and can be "cured" through the application of behavioral and other appropriate forms of therapy.

_____ 12-27. The belief that correctional treatment programs have had little success in rehabilitating offenders.

_____ 12-28. A sentencing style which represents a movement away from traditional confinement options and an increased use of correctional resources which are available in the community.

_____ 12-29. A prison program in which inmates are temporarily released into the community in order to meet job responsibilities.

_____ 12-30. An imprisonment strategy based upon the desire to prevent recurrent crime but which has abandoned any hope of rehabilitation.

DISCUSSION EXERCISES

Sentencing Philosophies and Prison Eras

Match the sentencing goal with the prison era that most closely approximates that goal. Explain your reasoning.

Retribution	Penitentiary Era (1790-1825)
General Deterrence	Mass Prison Stage (1825-1876)
Specific Deterrence	Reformatory stage (1876-1890)
Rehabilitation	Industrial Prison Era (1890-1935)
Incapacitation	Punitive Era (1935-1945)
Restoration	Era of Treatment (1945-1967)
	Community-based Decarceration (1967-1980)
	Warehousing/Overcrowding (1980-1995)
	Just Deserts (1995-present)

Which Is More Humane—Corporal Punishment or Incarceration?

The Quakers originally intended the penitentiary to be a more humane alternative to corporal punishment. Some critics argue that the deprivation of liberty for an ever-increasing period of time is a harsher punishment because of its psychological damage to the offender. Indeed, parenting authorities are still arguing the merits of subjecting a child to "time out" (or being sent to his or her room, or grounded) as opposed to a quick spanking (that is over within minutes). Should we begin to discuss the reintroduction of corporal punishment for some offenses? What form would corporal punishment take today? Singapore and other countries still utilize corporal punishment, and indeed the United States didn't completely abolish whipping until the early 1970s.

Private Prisons - Pros and "Cons"

Although they haven't been as successful as they had hoped, many private companies such as Corrections Corporation of America and Corrections Concepts have been able to convince state and federal prison authorities to turn over the operation of some prisons (or prison functions) to private vendors. If this trend continues, how will this impact the prison population of the next decade? How has privatization affected other public institutions, such as education or health care? Should the government be abdicating such basic responsibilities as the punishment of wrongdoers, the education of children, or the care of the sick?

CHAPTER

PRISON LIFE

CHAPTER SUMMARY

Chapter 13 provides a glimpse into the world of prison, from the point of view of both inmates and guards. A review of a variety of research studies detailing prison life is provided, along with a discussion of Goffman's concept of Total Institutions. In a prison setting, this prisonization process leads to the creation of a prison subculture, complete with a unique vocabulary that allows inmates to more easily describe certain types of offenders.

A discussion of prison society leads to Gresham Sykes' contention that the pains of imprisonment shape the experience of offenders, leading to the creation of deprivation model. Inmates are deprived of liberty, goods and services, heterosexual relationships, autonomy, and personal security, and the prison subculture is an adaptation to these five restricted areas. A detailed discussion of inmate life and the evolution of subcultures follows, including an examination of homosexuality in prison, and some of the prison lifestyles that have emerged. Inmate types include: the mean dude; the hedonist; the opportunist; the retreatist; the legalist; the radical; the colonist; the religious; and the realist.

Prison staff must also cope with the restrictive environment of prison, and their primary emphasis is on custody and control of the inmate population. Correctional officers are also categorized in the book, with prevalent types including the dictator, the friend, the merchant, the indifferent, the climber, and the reformer. Testing and training of correctional officers is also discussed.

A section on prison riots is included, with a brief history of some of the more spectacular riots in recent history, an analysis of the causes of riots, and an outline of the stages of riots.

The life of female offenders is explored, with an examination of the issues that are most pressing for women inmates, the characteristics of female offenders, the social structure of women's prisons, the typology of women inmates, and the role of violence in female institutions.

The legal aspects of prison are also discussed, with an examination of such concepts as the hands-off doctrine prevalent until the 1960s, and civil death. The balancing test established in 1974 with the case of *Pell* v. *Procunier* is detailed, as well as an outline of the various constitutional issues that have been challenged related to inmate rights in the last 30 years. The areas outlined include religious freedom, freedom of speech and communication, access to legal assistance, medical treatment, protection from harm and abuse; and institutional punishment and discipline. The grievance procedures currently in place are discussed, as well as the increase in the prevalence of prisoner unions.

Finally, the special issues facing correctional administrators in recent years are examined. These include the very real threat of AIDS, the increasing number of older inmates, and the special needs of mentally ill inmates.

LEARNING TIPS

STUDY SESSIONS

Avoid scheduling long study sessions. Four two-hour study sessions are far more productive than one eight-hour session. The amount of time actually spent productively in excessively long study sessions is very small. However, if long study sessions are inevitable, be sure to give your mind and body a break for a few minutes each hour. Also, be sure to study a variety of subjects. Studying similar subjects back to back is usually unproductive.

READING AND OUTLINING

When reading material, utilize the textbook's chapter outline or create an outline yourself to help guide your way through the information as you progress through the reading. Make the outlines more complete by adding headlines, notes, and thoughts. Whether using traditional Roman numeral outlines or your own methodology, outlining makes difficult material more understandable and allows you to see the larger picture rather than getting caught up in insignificant details or trivia.

KEY TERMS

Total Institutions: Enclosed facilities, generally separated from society both physically and socially, where the inhabitants share all aspects of their lives on a daily basis.

Prison Subculture: The values and behavioral patterns characteristic of prison inmates. Prison subculture has been found to have surprising consistencies across the country.

Prisonization: The process whereby institutionalized individuals come to accept prison lifestyles and criminal values.

Prison Argot: The slang characteristic of prison subcultures and prison life.

Hands-off Doctrine: A historical policy of nonintervention with regard to prison management which American courts tended to follow until the late 1960s.

Civil Death: The legal status of prisoners in some jurisdictions who are denied the opportunity to vote, hold public office, marry, or enter into contracts by virtue of their status as incarcerated felons.

Grievance Procedure: Formalized arrangements, usually involving a neutral hearing board, whereby institutionalized individuals have the opportunity to register complaints about the conditions of their confinement.

Balancing Test: A principle developed by the courts, and applied to the corrections arena by the 1974 case of *Pell* v. *Procunier*, which attempts to weigh the rights of an individual as guaranteed by the Constitution, against the authority of states to make laws or otherwise restrict a person's freedom in order to protect its interests and its citizens.

Example: Prison administrators routinely read the mail of inmates, censoring material that they consider to be detrimental to the security of the institution.

Writ of Habeas Corpus: The writ which directs the person detaining a prisoner to bring him or her before a judicial officer to determine the lawfulness of the imprisonment.

KEY CASES

Pell v. *Procunier* (1974): The U.S. Supreme Court established a "balancing test" which served to guide prison authorities in determining what rights an inmate should have. Inmates should have the same rights as non-incarcerated citizens, provided that the legitimate needs of the prison for security, custody, and safety are not compromised.

Procunier v. *Martinez* (1974): A prisoner's mail may be censored if it is necessary to do so for security purposes.

Houchins v. *KQED* (1978): News personnel cannot be denied correspondence with inmates, but they have no constitutional right to interview inmates or inspect correctional facilities beyond what is available to the general public.

Wolff v. *McDonnell* (1974): Sanctions cannot be levied against inmates without appropriate due process. Beginning of concept of "state-created liberty interests."

Block v. *Rutherford* (1984): In the interests of security, jails can prohibit all visits from friends and relatives.

Johnson v. *Avery* (1968): Inmates have a right to consult "jail-house lawyers" for advice if assistance from trained legal professionals is not available.

Estelle v. *Gamble* (1976): Requires prison officials to provide for inmates' medical care and established the concept of "deliberate indifference" in determining whether or not prison administrators are meeting the medical needs of prisoners.

Bounds v. *Smith* (1977): Not only confirmed the right of prisoners to have access to the courts and to legal assistance, but also required states to assist inmates in the preparation and filing of legal papers. This assistance can be given through trained personnel or through the creation and availability of a law library for inmates.

Newman v. *Alabama* (1972): Found Alabama's prison medical services to be so inadequate as to be "shocking to the conscience."

Ruiz v. *Estelle* (1982): Challenged the structure of the Texas prison system and specifically required major changes in the handling of inmate medical care. The court ordered an improvement in record keeping, physical facilities, and general medical care, while it continued to monitor the progress of the department.

Hudson v. *Palmer* (1984): The need for prison officials to conduct thorough and unannounced searches precludes inmates' right to privacy in personal possessions.

Jones v. *North Carolina Prisoner's Union* (1977): Prisons must establish some formal opportunity for the airing of inmate grievances.

Cruz v. *Beto* (1972): Inmates must be given a "reasonable opportunity" to pursue their religious faith, even if it differs from traditional forms of worship.

Helling v. *McKinney* (1993): Inmate sued due to involuntary exposure to second-hand ciga-rette smoke. Court indicated that prison officials are responsible not only for "inmates' cur-rent serious health problems," but also for maintaining environmental conditions under which health problems might be prevented from developing.

Sandin v. *Conner* (1995): An apparent return to the hands-off doctrine when the Court rejected the argument that any state action taken for a punitive reason encroaches upon a prisoner's constitutional due process right to be free from the deprivation of liberty.

PRACTICE TEST QUESTIONS

MULTIPLE CHOICE

13-1. _____ develop independently of the plans of prison administrators.
   a. Prison subcultures
   b. Total institutions
   c. Women's prisons
   d. Parole boards

13-2. Prison guards are generally considered to be part of the _____ staff in prisons.
   a. professional
   b. administrative
   c. custodial
   d. treatment
   e. none of the above

13-3. The policy followed by the courts until the 1960's in refusing to hear inmate com-plaints about the conditions of incarceration and the constitutional deprivations of inmate life was called the
   a. "hands off" doctrine.
   b. inmate code.
   c. "fingers crossed" model.
   d. Bloody Codes.
   e. "deliberate indifference" policy.

13-4. The 1969 federal court decision in *Holt* v. *Sarver* declared the entire prison system in the state of _____ to be in violation of the constitutional ban against cruel and unusual punishment.
   a. Indiana
   b. New York
   c. Arkansas
   d. New Mexico
   e. Texas

13-5. The _____ established by the U.S. Supreme Court in the 1974 case of *Pell* v. *Procunier* has served as a guideline generally applicable to all prison operations.
   a. either-or doctrine
   b. balancing test
   c. writ of habeas corpus
   d. prisonization process
   e. none of the above

13-6. In the argot of prisons, an inmate who uses force to take what he wants from others is referred to as a
   a. rat.
   b. gorilla.

c. merchant.

d. fish.

e. punk.

13-7. In *The Society of Captives*, Gresham Sykes claims that prisoners are deprived of all of the following except:

a. liberty.

b. goods and services.

c. homosexual relationships.

d. autonomy.

e. personal security.

13-8. Inmates adapt a series of lifestyles in an attempt to survive the prison experience. _____ build their lifestyle around the limited pleasures which can be had within the confines of prison.

a. mean dudes

b. hedonists

c. opportunists

d. retreatists

e. colonists

13-9. Correctional officers can be classified according to certain categories. If an officer tries to fraternize with inmates, attempting to be "one of the guys," he would be classified as a(n) _____.

a. dictator

b. friend

c. merchant

d. indifferent

e. fraternizer

13-10. All of the following are listed as contributing to the "graying" of America's prison population except:

a. increasing crime among those over 50.

b. the gradual aging of the society from which prisoners come.

c. a trend toward longer sentences.

d. the reduction in the number of older habitual offenders in prison.

TRUE–FALSE

_____ 13-11. In 1935 an Indiana University Sociology professor completed a ground-breaking study of prison life when he voluntarily served three months in prison as a participant-observer, to discover what being an inmate was really like.

_____ 13-12. Prison argot is a secret language prisoners use to communicate that no one except the prisoners know.

_____ 13-13. In all state and federal prison facilities combined, the number of incarcerated male prisoners is larger than the number of incarcerated female prisoners by a ratio of slightly more than 2 to 1.

_____ 13-14. The "Chivalry Factor" lead to a recent decline in the number of women sentenced to prison, as more and more judges are reluctant to separate mothers from their children.

_____ 13-15. Few states have any substantial capacity for the psychiatric treatment of mentally disturbed inmates.

_____ 13-16. The U.S. Supreme Court case of *Hudson* v. *Palmer* (1984) asserted that the need for prison officials to conduct thorough and unannounced searches is greater than inmates' right to privacy in personal possessions.

_____ 13-17. A prisoner's private mail from immediate family members may not be opened and censored by prison authorities.

_____ 13-18. Prison riots are generally unplanned and tend to occur spontaneously, the result of some relatively minor precipitating event.

_____ 13-19. Most male sexual aggressors in prisons do not consider themselves to be heterosexual.

_____ 13-20. Inmates have a right to consult "jail house lawyers" for advice if assistance from trained legal professionals is not provided by the prison.

MATCHING

a. total institutions
b. prison subculture
c. hands-off doctrine
d. prisonization
e. prison argot
f. writ of *habeas corpus*

g. civil death
h. balancing test
i. *Cruz* v. *Beto*
j. *Johnson* v. *Avery*
k. *Bounds* v. *Smith*
l. grievance procedures

_____ 13-21. The slang characteristic of prison subcultures and prison life.

_____ 13-22. Enclosed facilities where the inhabitants share all aspects of their lives on a daily basis.

_____ 13-23. A principle developed by the courts which attempts to weigh the rights of an individual as guaranteed by the Constitution, against the authority of states to make laws in order to protect its interests and its citizens.

_____ 13-24. The values and behavioral patterns characteristic of prison inmates.

_____ 13-25. A historical policy of non-intervention with regard to prison management which American courts tended to follow until the late 1960s.

_____ 13-26. The process whereby institutionalized individuals come to accept prison lifestyles and criminal values.

_____ 13-27. The legal status of prisoners in some jurisdictions who are denied the opportunity to vote, hold public office, marry, or enter into contracts by virtue of their status as incarcerated felons.

_____ 13-28. Case which required that inmates must be given a "reasonable opportunity" to pursue their religious faith even if it differs from traditional forms of worship.

_____ 13-29. Formalized arrangements whereby prisoners have the opportunity to register complaints about the conditions of their confinement.

_____ 13-30. The legal document which directs the person detaining a prisoner to bring him or her before a judicial officer to determine the lawfulness of the imprisonment.

DISCUSSION EXERCISES

Redesigning Prisons

You have been asked to serve on a statewide commission on criminal justice and corrections, and the commission's primary task is to design a new, more effective correctional facility. You should consider the following factors and any others that you deem important.

1. Architectural design, size, location, and physical layout
2. Inmate population (size and type)

3. Staffing needs
4. Inmate rights and self-government
5. Educational, vocational, religious, recreational, and training needs
6. Medical, psychological, and counseling services
7. Connections to the community and contacts with the outside world
8. Release arrangements
9. Grievance procedures
10. Funding
11. Other factors

You will be asked to present your correctional plan to the state legislative subcommittee responsible for corrections. You should be prepared to discuss the major strengths and weaknesses of your proposal.

The legislature is thrilled with your idea. Now they want you to sell it to the local community where the correctional center will be located. Present your proposal to the citizens gathered at a town forum to persuade them to accept your proposal.

Prison Subculture v. Student Subculture

Your text outlines in great detail the adaptation process that inmates go through in creating a place for themselves in the prison setting. How does this differ from the adaptation process and social types in a traditional high school or university? Do students adapt certain postures or fall into categories that can be easily identified? What about prison argot? Do students ever use a shorthand way of describing other students, teachers, or administrators? Explain.

Inmate Types

The text provides sketches of a variety of prison lifestyles that offenders may try to use to adapt to their stay behind bars. How might the case studies we examined earlier in the bail decision making exercise fit into the inmate types described? What additional information might you need to know to make a more informed decision?

1. Salvadore Lopez, is a 52-year-old farm worker who cannot read. He has a wife and two children. Lopez was charged with smuggling guns, marijuana, and other narcotics across the Mexican border. The prosecutor, when discussing the case with the news media, says that he suspects Mr. Lopez of being a person who has been transporting guns and drugs for years, but who, until now, has avoided being arrested by authorities. Mr. Lopez claims that he is completely innocent

2. Roger A. Kearney, is a 27-year-old electrical engineer. He is charged with vehicular homicide stemming from the death of Chris Pariano. Pariano was stepping out of his pickup truck when Kearney sped down the wrong side of the street. Kearney was drunk at the time, police said. The police also learned that he had eight previous convictions for drunk driving and 19 other serious vehicular offenses.

3. Edward Savitz is a 50-year-old single man who has a good-paying full-time job and lives in an expensive high-rise apartment. He is charged with the statutory rape of a 16-year-old, sexual abuse of two others, and corrupting the morals of a minor. It is alleged that he paid to have sex with hundreds of boys, but on all occasions, the young men agreed to participate. The maximum sentence that he can receive for his crimes is 5 to 10 years. Mr. Savitz has been diagnosed as having the AIDS virus.

4. At the age of 19, Frank Anderson was convicted of rape and sentenced to prison for three years. Approximately one year after his release, he became a suspect in a number of robberies of older men. He threatened a number of the victims with bodily harm if they filed complaints. One 71-year-old victim nevertheless agreed to cooperate with the authorities. Based on his complaint, Anderson was arrested and charged with robbery.

Shortly after his first appearance, he was released on bail. Anderson then broke into the 71-year-old man's house, beat him, kicked him numerous times, and stole $3,000 and a gun. The victim suffered a concussion and needed seven stitches. Anderson was identified and again apprehended, and was charged with an additional count of robbery. Again, he was released on bail for $1,500. Anderson returned to the home of the victim, assaulted him, and attempted to stop him from cooperating with the police. He was once again apprehended and this time charged with aggravated battery.

5. An 18-year-old girl, Kim Walak, was arrested for shoplifting. She claimed to be indigent, with no steady source of income. She lived with an unemployed boyfriend, and she dropped out of school in the 11th grade. She had one prior arrest for shoplifting, but those charges were dismissed for unknown reasons.

C H A P T E R

JUVENILE DELINQUENCY

CHAPTER SUMMARY

Chapter 14 examines the specific issue area of juvenile delinquency. Juvenile crime is a perplexing problem for the criminal justice system. It is perplexing because research indicates that the amount of serious crime committed by juveniles is increasing. The public has demanded a strict response because of the escalating crime rate and newsworthy crimes committed by juveniles. However, the public's desire for a juvenile crime crackdown, and the demand that juvenile punishments are equivalent to adult punishments, is inconsistent with the underlying philosophy of the juvenile court. The philosophy is that the system should make decisions that are in the best interests of the child.

This chapter examines four areas of juvenile delinquency: first, it examines the historical development of the juvenile justice system; second, it compares the juvenile justice system to the adult system; third, it discusses the juvenile justice system process and finally, it discusses several criticisms of the juvenile system.

The text discusses the historical beginnings of the juvenile justice system throughout the world and in America and traces this history through several important U.S. Supreme Court cases decided in the 1970s and 1980s. The text exams the historical evolution of the juvenile justice system, beginning with a discussion of how juveniles in earliest times were not treated differently than adults. For example, the laws of King Aethelbert made no special provisions for offenders because of age. The common law principle of *parens patriae* is important to an understanding of juvenile justice because it means that the state can assume the role of the parent and take custody of a child.

In America, the criminal justice response to juveniles began in the early nineteenth century with the development of houses of refuge. The **child savers movement** began in the mid-1800s, influencing the development of reform schools. The early model, embodied in the **Chicago Reform School**, focused on emulating family environments to provide security and build moral character, emphasizing traditional values, such as hard work. Finally, The text discusses the beginnings of the juvenile court era from early legislation in Massachusetts and New York to the Illinois juvenile law that was modeled by most states to the federal government's Juvenile Court Act. Most legislation included six categories of children subject to the jurisdiction of the juvenile court: **delinquent children, undisciplined children, dependent children, neglected children, abused children**, and **status offenders**.

Chapter 14 then discusses several theoretical explanations for juvenile delinquency. This discussion includes Shaw and McKay's **social ecology approach**, Cloward and Ohlin's **opportunity theory**, and Sykes and Matza's **neutralization techniques**. Moreover, he discusses two significant research efforts to identify the determinants of delinquency. First, he discusses research conducted by Marvin Wolfgang that traced the delinquent behavior of a birth cohort in Philadelphia. Second, he discusses the Program of Research on the Causes and Correlates of Juvenile Delinquency and its three coordinated projects.

Chapter 14 also provides an excellent overview of several significant court decisions affecting juveniles. The most significant is *In Re Gault*. This court decision guaranteed several procedural rights to juveniles including the right to have notice of the charges, right to counsel, right to confront and cross-examine witnesses, and the right to appeal. Other cases discussed include *In Re Winship*, *McKeiver* v. *Pennsylvania*, *Breed* v. *Jones*, *Kent* v. *United States*, and *Schall* v. *Martin*. Juveniles, however, are not provided all of the same protections guaranteed to adult defendants. For example, juveniles do not have a constitutional right to a jury trial.

The juvenile justice system, as a process, involves four stages: **intake, adjudication, disposition**, and **postadjudication review**. **Intake** involves the filing of a juvenile petition by some party, such as the police, alleging illegal behavior by the juvenile. **Adjudication** is the trial process for juveniles. Adjudicatory hearings are similar to the adult trial, but with some exceptions. A **dispositional** hearing, similar to an adult sentencing hearing, occurs to determine the action the court should take against a juvenile. Judges have several options at disposition, including outright release, probation, or confinement to a secure institution.

Chapter 14 concludes with the future of the juvenile justice system, acknowledging that it will likely undergo significant reforms because of criticism, including increasing penalties, reducing privacy, and eliminating diversionary opportunities.

LEARNING TIP

NOTE REVIEW

With short-term memory failing very quickly, it is important in note taking to review your notes as soon as possible, especially within 24 hours. Extensively review your notes, correct misspellings, write out abbreviations, insert any information you were unable to write in your notes during the class, and make your writing as legible as possible. While reviewing your notes immediately can save valuable time when studying for tests, it also helps transfer information from short-term to long-term memory.

KEY TERMS

Juvenile Justice System: Government agencies which function to investigate, supervise, adjudicate, care for, or confine youthful offenders and other children subject to the jurisdiction of the court.

Delinquency: Juvenile actions or conduct in violation of criminal law, juvenile status offenses, and other juvenile misbehavior.

> Example: Mary Rose's recent encounters with the law include two shoplifting offenses, a truancy charge, and a violation of curfew. All are considered delinquency.

Parens Patriae: A common law principle which allows the state to assume a parental role and to take custody of a child when he or she becomes delinquent, is abandoned, or is in need of care which the natural parents are unable or unwilling to do.

Delinquent Child: A child who has engaged in activity which would be considered a crime if the child were an adult. The term "delinquent" is applied to such a child in order to avoid the stigma which comes from application of the term "criminal."

Example: A child that commits a murder is a delinquent.

Undisciplined Child: A child who is beyond parental control, as evidenced by his or her refusal to obey legitimate authorities such as school officials and teachers.

Dependent Child: A child who has no parent(s) or whose parent(s) is (are) unable to care for him or for her.

Neglected Child: A child is not receiving the proper level of physical or psychological care from his or her parent(s) or guardians(s) or who has been placed up for adoption in violation of the law.

Example: Jane Doe, estimated to be about two-weeks-old, was found wrapped in a blanket and left in a trash can. Jane would be classified as a neglected child.

Abused Child: A child who has been physically, sexually, or mentally abused. Most states also consider a child abused who is forced into delinquent activity by a parent or guardian.

Example: A child forced to be a prostitute by her mother would be considered an abused child.

Status Offense: An act or conduct which is declared by statute to be an offense, but only when committed by or engaged in by a juvenile, and which can be adjudicated only by a juvenile court.

Example: Incorrigibility and truancy are typical status offenses.

Status Offender: A child who commits an act which is contrary to the law by virtue of the juvenile's status as a child. Purchasing cigarettes, buying alcohol, and truancy are examples of such behavior.

Social Ecology: An approach which focused on the misbehavior of lower-class youth and saw delinquency primarily as the result of social disorganization.

Social Disorganization: A condition which is said to exist when a group is faced with social change, uneven cultural development, maladaptiveness, disharmony, conflict, and lack of consensus.

Opportunity Theory: A perspective which sees delinquency as the result of limited legitimate opportunities for success available to most lower-class youth.

Cohort: A group of individuals sharing similarities of age, place of birth, and residence. Cohort analysis is a social scientific technique by which such groups are tracked over time in order to identify unique and observable behavioral traits which characterize them.

Juvenile Petition: A document filed in juvenile court alleging that a juvenile is delinquent, a status offender, or a dependent, and asking that the court assume jurisdiction over the juvenile or asking that an alleged delinquent be transferred to a criminal court for prosecution as an adult.

Intake: The first step in decision making regarding a juvenile whose behavior or alleged behavior is in violation of the law or which could otherwise cause a juvenile court to assume jurisdiction.

Adjudicatory Hearing: The courtroom stage of a juvenile hearing, which is similar in substance to a criminal hearing or trial.

Dispositionary Hearing: The final stage in the processing of adjudicated juveniles, in which a decision is made on the form of treatment or penalty which should be imposed upon the child.

Juvenile Disposition: The decision of a juvenile court, concluding a disposition hearing, that an adjudicated juvenile be committed to a juvenile correctional facility, or be placed in a juvenile residence, shelter, or care or treatment program, or be required to meet certain standards of conduct, or be released.

PRACTICE TEST QUESTIONS

MULTIPLE CHOICE

14-1. Which of the following was not emphasized by the reform school movement?
   a. traditional family values
   b. the worth of hard work
   c. wholesome family environments
   d. affection necessary to build moral character
   e. all of the above were emphasized by the reform school movement

14-2. _____ children are defined as those who do not receive proper care from their parents or guardians.
   a. Dependent
   b. Neglected
   c. Abused
   d. Undisciplined

14-3. Which of the following is not a status offense?
   a. truancy
   b. running away from home
   c. robbery
   d. incorrigibility
   e. all of the above are status offenses

14-4. Which of the following U.S. Supreme Court cases ruled that juveniles are entitled to representation by attorneys who must have access to their records when being transferred to adult court?
   a. *Breed* v. *Jones*
   b. *Schall* v. *Martin*
   c. *Kent* v. *U.S.*
   d. *Ex parte Crouse*

14-5. Which of the following theories sees delinquency as the result of social disorganization?
   a. social ecology
   b. opportunity
   c. neutralization
   d. strain

14-6. Which of the following is a protective factor that strengthens juveniles so that they do not become delinquent?
   a. commitment to school
   b. achievement at school
   c. high levels of parental supervision
   d. high levels of attachment to parents
   e. all of the above

14-7. What is the evidentiary standard that must be established at a delinquency hearing?
   a. preponderance of the evidence
   b. beyond a reasonable doubt
   c. in most instances
   d. the feel good standard

14-8. Which of the following steps of the juvenile court process is similar to an adult trial?
    a. intake
    b. adjudication
    c. disposition
    d. postadjudicatory review

14-9. _____ is a common law principle which allows the state to assume a parental role and to take custody of a child when he or she becomes delinquent, is abandoned, or is in need of care which the natural parents are unable or unwilling to do.
    a. Arrest
    b. Community outreach
    c. *Parens patriae*
    d. Intake

14-10. The first juvenile court was created in 1899 in
    a. Indiana
    b. Illinois
    c. New York
    d. Ohio
    e. Florida

TRUE–FALSE

_____ 14-11. The laws of King Aethelbert created our current juvenile justice system by allowing special allowances for the age of the offender.

_____ 14-12. Gresham Sykes and David Matza developed opportunity theory in the 1960s, arguing that delinquency resulted from the lack of legitimate opportunities for success available to most lower-class youth.

_____ 14-13. Violence among teenagers and teenage suicide continue to decrease at a rapid rate.

_____ 14-14. Very few juvenile correctional institutions are overcrowded.

_____ 14-15. Juveniles have a constitutional right to a trial by jury.

_____ 14-16. A delinquent child is one who has no parents or whose parents are unable to care for him or for her.

_____ 14-17. Juvenile trials are open to the public and to the news media.

_____ 14-18. A juvenile's guilt must be proven beyond a reasonable doubt if charged with a criminal offense.

_____ 14-19. Juveniles charged with a status offense have the same procedural rights afforded to adults charged with a criminal offense.

_____ 14-20. A juvenile's record may be destroyed after he or she reaches a certain age.

MATCHING

a. status offender
b. dependent child
c. undisciplined child
d. neglected child
e. abused child
f. delinquent child
g. social disorganization
h. opportunity
i. *parens patriae*
j. judicial oversight
k. juvenile petition
l. indictment

_____ 14-21. A child who is beyond parental control, as evidenced by his or her refusal to obey legitimate authorities such as school officials and teachers.

_____ 14-22. A theory which views delinquency as the result of limited legitimate avenues to be successful.

_____ 14-23. Term applied to a child in order to avoid the stigma which comes from application of the term "criminal."

_____ 14-24. In some jurisdictions, a child who has been forced into delinquent activity by a parent or guardian.

_____ 14-25. A child who has no parents.

_____ 14-26. A principle which allows the state to assume a parental role.

_____ 14-27. A document filed in juvenile court alleging that a juvenile is delinquent, a status offender, or a dependent.

_____ 14-28. A child who commits an act which is contrary to the law by virtue of the juvenile's status as a child.

_____ 14-29. A condition which is said to exist when a group is faced with social change, uneven cultural development, maladaptiveness, disharmony, conflict, and lack of consensus.

_____ 14-30. A child is not receiving the proper level of physical or psychological care from his or her parents.

DISCUSSION EXERCISES

1. Should the juvenile justice system be abolished? Why or why not?

2. Judge Gayle Garner has the following three juvenile cases on her docket:
   a. Jarred Jeter is a 17-year-old high-school drop out. He has recently been convicted of two burglaries. His criminal record includes three other crimes: two shoplifting incidents and a theft. His parents are frustrated his behavior and admit having trouble controlling him. Jarred's two brothers are well behaved and have no criminal records.
   b. Anne Yeerns is 15 years old and was convicted of attempting to steal a car. This was her first offense. However, she is also a runaway. On two prior occasions, she has run away from her father. The first time she went back home after 3 days, the second time the police brought her back after one week, and this time she claims she was stealing the car to get as far away as possible. Anne's father did not attend the dispositional hearing.
   c. Patrick Darvy is 12-years-old, and was recently initiated into a juvenile gang. He was caught selling drugs; it was his first offense. Patrick lives with his mother, who is divorced. Miss Darvy is very concerned about recent changes in his behavior and would like the courts help in changing his behavior.

   Make a recommendation to Judge Garner for the dispositions of these three cases. Discuss what sentence you would recommend, and provide the rationale for your recommendation.

C   H   A   P   T   E   R

DRUGS AND CRIME

CHAPTER SUMMARY

The text examines the important issue of drugs and crime in Chapter 15. Drug use, drug-related crime, drug laws, and drug enforcement efforts significantly affect processes of criminal justice. A large proportion of the financial and personnel resources of the criminal justice system are used to respond to the drug problem in America. Police departments utilize undercover operations increasing the number of arrests of drug offenders. Court dockets are overwhelmed by prosecutions for drug offenses. The number of defendants incarcerated for drug offenses continues to grow.

Chapter 15 begins with an overview of the drug problem in America. First, it illustrates the importance of the topic by highlighting the specific impacts of drugs on the system. He also provides essential background information with a discussion of what is a drug. He also examines alcohol abuse and the criminal justice system's response to alcohol-related offenses.

The text then traces the history of drug abuse covering the use of **opium, morphine**, and **heroin** in the 1800s and early 1990s, the response to **marijuana** in the 1900s, the use of **LSD** in the 1960s and 1970s, and the use of **crack cocaine** in the 1980s. He then discusses the corresponding history of drug abuse legislation in America. The first significant piece of federal anti-drug legislation was the **Harrison Act of 1914**. He also explains the **Marijuana Tax Act of 1937**, the **Narcotic Control Act of 1956**, the **Comprehensive Drug Abuse Prevention and Control Act of 1970**, and the **Anti-Drug Abuse Act of 1988**. This latter piece of legislation created the position of "**drug czar**" within the **Office of National Drug Control Policy**.

A detailed explanation of three major drug types, **marijuana, cocaine**, and **heroin,** is next. He describes how these drugs are produced, consumed, and trafficked into the United States. Cocaine, for example, is extracted from the leaves of the coca plant. It produces intense psychological effects and typically enters the United States from Peru, Bolivia, Columbia, or Ecuador.

Chapter 15 then examines social problems related to the drug problem. The text discusses the link between drugs and crime, money laundering efforts, narcoterrorism, lost productivity, and police corruption. For example, there are at least three dimensions to our understanding of the links between drugs and crime. First, crimes specifically related to the use or sale of drugs. Second, crimes committed by drug users, such as the addict that commits robberies to maintain her habit. Third, the organized criminal and gang activities that support the drug trade.

Chapter 15 concludes with a discussion of various criminal justice strategies used to respond to the drug problem. These strategies have very different philosophical orientations. On the one hand, several methods are discussed that focus on the supply side of drug use. **Strict enforcement**, **forfeiture**, **interdiction**, and **crop control efforts** concentrate on responding to the problem by attacking the selling of drugs by increasing efforts by police, courts, and correctional institutions. Strict enforcement efforts include the **zero tolerance policy** of the U.S. Coast Guard, calls for harsher punishments, and increasing the number of police officers responding to the problem. **Forfeiture** involves seizing the assets of individuals involved in drug trafficking, and interdiction involves international efforts to prevent drugs from entering the United States or destroying crops. On the other hand, education, treatment, and counseling efforts focus on prevention and the drug user. For example, project DARE attempts to educate school children, focusing on decision-making skills, peer pressure, and choosing alternatives. The chapter concludes with a discussion of legalization and decriminalization efforts.

LEARNING TIP

MULTIPLE CHOICE QUESTIONS

Whenever you are not penalized for wrong answers on multiple-choice questions and you are completely unable to answer the question, there are three ways to choose the best answer: First, eliminate any answer you know to be wrong. Second, if two answers are very similar, except for a couple of words, choose one of these two answers. Third, if it is a question involving numbers and the answers are spread out in numerical order, choose an answer that lies in the middle.

KEY TERMS

Drug Abuse: Illicit drug use that results in social, economic, psychological, or legal problems for the user Source: Bureau of Justice Statistics, *Drugs, Crimes and the Justice System* (Washington, D.C.: BJS, 1992, p. 20).

Controlled Substance: A specifically defined bioactive or psychoactive chemical substance which is proscribed by law.

Drug: Any chemical substance defined by social convention as bio- or psychoactive.

Psychoactive Substance: A chemical substance which affects cognition, feeling, and/or awareness.

Recreational Drug User: A person who uses drugs relatively infrequently and whose use occurs primarily among friends and within social contexts which define drug use as pleasurable. Most addicts began as recreational users.

Physical Addiction (or Physical Dependence): A biologically based craving for a specific drug, which results from frequent use of the substance. Dependence upon drugs is marked by a growing tolerance of a drug's effects so that increased amounts of a drug are needed to obtain a desired effect and by the onset of withdrawal symptoms over periods of prolonged abstinence. Source: Bureau of Justice Statistics, *Drugs, Crime, and the Justice System* (Washington, D.C.: BJS, 1992, p. 21).

Harrison Act: The first major piece of federal antidrug legislation, passed in 1914.

Controlled Substances Act: Title II of the Comprehensive Drug Abuse Prevention and Control Act of 1970, which established schedules classifying psychotic drugs according to their degree of psychoactivity.

Drug Czar: The head of the Office of National Drug Control Policy (ONDCP). A federal cabinet-level position that was originally created during the years of the Reagan presidency to organize federal drug-fighting efforts.

Money Laundering: The process of converting illegally earned assets, originating as cash, to one or more alternative forms to conceal such incriminating factors as illegal origin and true ownership. Source: Clifford Karchmer and Douglas Ruch, "State and Local Money Laundering Control Strategies," *NIJ Research in Brief* (Washington, D.C.: NIJ, 1992, p. 1).

Narcoterrorism: A political alliance between terrorist organizations and drug-supplying cartels. The cartels provide financing for the terrorists, who in turn provide quasi-military protection to the drug dealers.

Forfeiture: The authorized seizure of money, negotiable instruments, securities, or other things of value. In federal anti-drug laws the authorization of judicial representatives to seize all moneys, negotiable instruments, securities, or other things of value furnished or intended to be furnished by any person in exchange for a controlled substance, and all proceeds traceable to such an exchange.

RICO: An acronym which stands for "Racketeer Influenced Corrupt Organization" and refers to a federal statute which allows for the federal seizure of assets derived from illegal enterprise.

Interdiction: The interception of drug traffic at the nation's borders. Interdiction is one of the many strategies used to stem the flow of illegal drugs in the United States.

Legalization: Eliminates the laws and associated criminal penalties that prohibit the production, sale, distribution, and possession of a controlled substance.

Decriminalization: The re-definition of certain criminal behaviors into regulated activities, which become "ticketable" rather than "arrestable."

PRACTICE TEST QUESTIONS

MULTIPLE CHOICE

15-1. Which of the following pieces of anti-drug abuse legislation required persons to register with the federal government and to pay a tax of $1.00 per year?
 a. The Harrison Act
 b. Marijuana Tax Act
 c. Narcotic Control Act
 d. Comprehensive Drug Abuse Prevention and Control Act
 e. Anti-Drug Abuse Act

15-2. The Anti-Drug Abuse Act of 1988 accomplished all of the following except:
 a. it increased penalties for "recreational" drug use.
 b. it made it difficult for suspected drug dealers to purchase weapons.
 c. it denied federal benefits to convicted drug offenders.
 d. it eliminated the possibility of capital punishment for drug-related murders.
 e. all of the above

15-3. _____ are psychoactive drugs with relatively mild effects whose potential for abuse and addiction is substantially low.

    a. Soft drugs

    b. Hard drugs

    c. Crack cocaine

    d. LSD

15-4. Zimring and Hawkins argue that current drug policy is based on three schools of thought. Which of these schools proposes that drug policy be built around a balancing of the social costs of drug abuse?

    a. public health generalism

    b. cost-benefit specifism

    c. legalist

    d. deterrence

15-5. Which of the following strategies focuses on reducing penalties for drug offenses, treating an offense similar to a traffic offense?

    a. legalization

    b. decriminalization

    c. crop control

    d. interdiction

15-6. Which of the following U.S. Supreme Court cases established the open fields doctrine?

    a. *Hester* v. *United States*

    b. *United States* v. *Dunn*

    c. *California* v. *Greenwood*

    d. *Abel* v. *United States*

15-7._____ is the involvement of insurgent groups in the trafficking of narcotics.

    a. Money laundering

    b. Forfeiture

    c. Narcoterrorism

    d. Pseudoterrorism

15-8. Which of the following is not a soft drug?

    a. marijuana

    b. peyote

    c. hashish

    d. tranquilizers

    e. all of the above

15-9. Which of the following pieces of legislation made marijuana a federally prohibited controlled substance?

    a. Marijuana Tax Act of 1937

    b. Narcotic Control Act of 1956

    c. The Boggs Act of 1951

    d. The Comprehensive Drug Abuse Prevention and Control Act

15-10. Under the Controlled Substances Act, cough medicine would be considered a

    a. Schedule I drug.

    b. Schedule II drug.

    c. Schedule III drug.

    d. Schedule IV drug.

    e. Schedule V drug.

15-11. Which U.S. Supreme Court case held that a warrantless search of a motel room after it is vacated is not unconstitutional?

    a. *Abel* v. *United States*

    b. *Oliver* v. *United States*

    c. *California* v. *Greenwood*

    d. *Ratzlaf* v. *United States*

TRUE–FALSE

_____ 15-12. The Marijuana Tax Act of 1937 created a special assistant to the president on drug issues to be known as a "drug czar."

_____ 15-13. Most federal prisoners are incarcerated for drug offenses.

_____ 15-14. Although use of hard drugs continues to increase, alcohol abuse is declining rapidly.

_____ 15-15. Abandoned property is protected under the Fourth Amendment provisions against search and seizure.

_____ 15-16. Most addicts begin as recreational users.

_____ 15-17. Cocaine is considered a soft drug by the criminal justice system, and crack is considered a hard drug.

_____ 15-18. Zimring and Hawkin's "Legalist" category suggests that drug control policies are necessary in order to prevent the collapse of social order and of society itself.

_____ 15-19. Because of the Anti-Drug Abuse Act of 1988, an offender that commits a drug-related murder can be sentenced to death.

_____ 15-20. Drug abuse has minimum social and personal costs beyond its impact on the criminal justice system.

MATCHING

a. the Harrison Act
b. forfeiture
c. RICO statute
d. anti-drug abuse act
e. interdiction
f. legalization
g. decriminalization
h. narcoterrorism
i. drug czar
j. Drug President
k. Controlled Substances Act
l. controlled substance
m. drug

_____ 15-21. A political alliance between terrorist organizations and drug-supplying cartels.

_____ 15-22. The interception of drug traffic at the nation's borders.

_____ 15-23. The re-definition of certain criminal behaviors into regulated activities, which become "ticketable" rather than "arrestable."

_____ 15-24. The authorized seizure of money, negotiable instruments, securities, or other things of value.

_____ 15-25. A federal cabinet-level position that was originally created during the years of the Reagan presidency to organize federal drug-fighting efforts.

_____ 15-26. Title II of the Comprehensive Drug Abuse Prevention and Control Act of 1970, which established schedules classifying psychotic drugs according to their degree of psychoactivity.

_____ 15-27. The first major piece of federal antidrug legislation, passed in 1914.

_____ 15-28. A specifically defined bioactive or psychoactive chemical substance which is proscribed by law.

_____ 15-29. Eliminates the laws and associated criminal penalties that prohibit the production, sale, distribution, and possession of a controlled substance.

_____ 15-30. Refers to legislation which allows for the federal seizure of assets derived from illegal enterprise.

DISCUSSION EXERCISES

1. What do you think of the concept of taxing drug suspects? How do you separate the tax collection efforts from law enforcement efforts? For example, suppose someone wanted to pay the excise tax on their illegal drugs. Aren't they admitting a crime simply by paying the tax? Wouldn't this be a violation of Fifth Amendment protections against self-incrimination? This concept is not new—Al Capone was eventually sentenced to prison not for being a notorious gangster, but for federal income tax evasion. Does the public interest in getting criminals off the street outweigh the individual's right to be safe from excessive government intervention?

2. A political consulting firm has requested your assistance in writing a memorandum on the pros and cons of the legalization of marijuana. Write an essay that discusses the advantages and disadvantages of the legalization of marijuana.

3. Historically, political policy on drug enforcement has approached the problem with one of two types of response. One response is to focus on cracking down on the sellers, increasing the number of arrests, and advocating for stricter punishments. The second response focuses on rehabilitating the user with treatment and counseling. Which approach, or combination of approaches, would you recommend as the most effective response to drugs? Discuss how this approach would impact the criminal justice system.

4. The war on drugs, fought through the 1980s and early 1990s, focused primarily on a strict enforcement approach. The strict enforcement approach provides police with wide latitude in formulating how best to respond to the drug problem. The conservative-minded U.S. Supreme Court has supported these efforts with several important court decisions that have limited the rights of individuals. For example, the Supreme Court has used several drug cases to help redefine Fourth Amendment protections against unreasonable search and seizures. The text discusses several of these cases. Your assignment is to discover these decisions and discuss the court's holding for each Fourth Amendment case.

DRUG TAX CHANGES ARE LONG OVERDUE
Bray's Efforts to Save the Law May Make It More Reasonable

Back in December, the Indiana Supreme Court issued a ruling on the state's law imposing an excise tax on illegal drugs that, if anything, made the situation even worse than it was.

Now an area legislator, State Sen. Richard Bray, R., Martinsville, is doing what he can to try to salvage something from the wreckage.

A number of years ago, when the War on Drugs was raging, the Legislature came up with what it thought was a really neat idea: Slap a $40-per gram "excise tax" on illegal drugs that people have to pay, or risk felony prosecution not only for possessing or dealing drugs but for not paying the tax.

The law was meant to lay a triple-whammy on illegal drugs: (1) normal prosecution for possession or dealing, (2) a heavy tax that the state Department of Revenue could automatically assess on drug possessors or dealers as soon as the amount of their stash was determined, and

(3) prosecution for nonpayment of the drug before they were caught.

The law had significant problems. Three area judges, all conservatives, had ruled before December that anyone paying it risked self-incrimination. And we have editorially noted a

basic problem with its fairness.

Under the law, if you had 29 ounces of marijuana, you paid no tax at all. But for 30 grams the tax was imposed—and the tax on 30 grams (one ounce) was $1,200—

with a 100 percent penalty for non-payment before arrest making it $2400. More dangerous drugs like cocaine, heroin, LSD, PCP, methaqualone, methcathinone and so forth that are sold in far smaller quantities thus were taxed less than marijuana, the least dangerous drug.

Then in December, the state Supreme Court ruled that the law amounted to double-jeopardy—double prosecution and punishment for the same crime. They rightly ruled that the tax is so severe that it amounts to a criminal punishment in itself. But then instead of just throwing out the tax, they held that anyone who had been assessed the tax by the state after their arrest—whether or not they had paid it—could not subsequently be charged, tried or convicted for drug possession or dealing because that prosecution would be a second punishment and hence double jeopardy.

That ruling has thrown thousands of pending drug prosecutions across the state into chaos, and has provided grounds for hundreds of convicted drug offenders to appeal to have their convictions voided. Many will walk out of prison as a result.

Now Bray, a former prosecutor, is attempting to gain passage of legislation that will undo some of the damage and redo the law to make it sensible.

Bray is seeking to amend the law to allow a judge to impose the tax at the time a drug offender is sen-

tenced, and not before. It also permits the state to collect the tax if a prosecutor has decided not to pursue charges against a drug suspect. That gets the cart (the tax) back behind the horse (the criminal prosecution), where it belongs.

Bray's amendment also reduces the tax to $3.50 per gram for marijuana. That's no magic figure; $2 or $5 or $10 per gram would be just as good. But at least it makes the tax on marijuana more commensurate with what it deserves to be, compared to that for far more dangerous drugs.

As it is, the tax is a bit silly as a revenue-generator. The state has levied drug taxes of $77 million since the law went into effect in July 1992, according to Revenue Department figures, but it has actually collected only $985,180 of that amount.

We would not mind seeing the entire tax concept dumped. Why not just continue seizing drug dealers' cash and cars for forfeiture and then impose massive fines on convicted drug dealers as part of their sentence once convicted?

But at least Bray's amendment would inject some common sense into the law—something the state justices' ruling didn't—and we hope it passes.

Reprinted with permission of the Herald-Times, Bloomington, IN

16

MULTINATIONAL CRIMINAL JUSTICE

CHAPTER SUMMARY

The chapter opens with an examination of the problems experienced by Asahara, the purported leader of a Japanese cult, in securing counsel to defend himself against charges that he masterminded a nerve gas attack in a Tokyo subway that killed 12 and injured more than 5,500 others. Unlike the U.S. legal defense community, which leaped to defend O.J. Simpson against murder charges, the Japanese attorneys are reluctant to take on such an infamous client. Japanese defense attorneys want to avoid the dishonor of representing a client who seemed so guilty of such a horrible crime.

Japan has been experiencing a dramatic increase in crime over the last few years, and explaining why this might be occurring is a good example of the work accomplished by **comparative criminologists**. These researchers examine the unique characteristics of crime in a variety of cultures and attempt to compare and contrast the differences and similarities that might exist. The chapter deals with a comparison of the justice systems in China, England, and the Islamic world. The role of international police agencies and the United Nations in the fight against crime worldwide is also examined.

The concept of **ethnocentrism** is important to the study of criminal justice. "Ethnocentric" means centered on one's own culture, and that tends to be the approach taken by most individuals. The assumption is made that one's own values and beliefs are superior to others. One of the other major problems in the field of comparative criminal justice is also touched upon: problems with the data utilized in examining the crime problem in other societies. The three biggest problems are (1) differences in defining crime, (2) diverse reporting practices, and (3) political and other influences on the reporting of statistics to international agencies.

The Chinese justice system is examined, with a brief discussion of the history of crime and criminal justice in the country. Under party Chairman Mao Zedong, the primary emphasis was on informal social control, and little emphasis was placed on formal bureaucratic structures. This model was based on the concept "Depend on the rule of man, not the rule of law." After Mao's death in 1976, reform began to creep into the country, and a much greater emphasis was placed on predictability and security. As it now stands, the Chinese Constitution contains 24 articles on the fundamental rights and duties of citizens, and guarantees equality before the law for all citizens. The jurisdiction of Chinese courts is similar to that of the United States, and the official crime rate in comparison to the United States is very low. One reason for this may be the reliance on **mediation committees,** which are civilian dispute resolution forums used to deal with a wide variety of conflicts. If a case cannot be handled by the mediation committee, Chinese criminal punishments can be quite severe, with an emphasis on lengthy prison sentences, and a much greater use of the death penalty for crimes ranging from publishing pornographic books to murder. The Chinese justice system has a heavy reliance on the concept of personal reformation, and the official recidivism rate is astonishingly low compared to Western cultures.

Islamic criminal justice is examined next. The Islamic concept of justice rests on four principles: (1) a sacred trust to be fair, (2) mutual respect for human beings, (3) a social bond which holds society together, and (4) a command from God. Crimes are divided into two categories, *Hudud* and *Tazirat*. *Hudud* crimes are serious violations of Islamic law and are regarded as offenses against God. These can include theft, adultery, drinking alcohol, and robbery. *Tazirat* crimes are minor violations of Islamic law, and are regarded as crimes against society, not God. These include murder, manslaughter, assault, and maiming. The Islamic courts have three levels, and appeals are relatively rare. Women are treated much differently from men and are considered inferior. The strict punishments handed down by Islamic courts seem bizarre to Westerners, but the crime rate in Islamic countries is very low by Western standards.

Criminal justice in England and Wales is also examined, and their systems come much closer to approximating the American experience with crime. The rates of crime and the reliance on statistics to track crime are similar to the United States. The British system is based on three documents: (1) the Magna Carta, (2) the Bill of Rights, and (3) the Act of Settlement. The Parliament serves as the legislative body, and laws passed cannot be challenged in the courts as they are in the United States. Also, there is no separation of the branches of government (such as executive, legislative, and judicial), and there are no state governments per se—everyone is subject to parliamentary law, with no local variations. The police, courts, and corrections subsystems are also discussed in some detail.

A variety of international criminal justice organizations are mentioned, most notably the International Society of Criminology (ISC). The United Nations has continued to play an important role in the area of international criminal justice, primarily by creating model legislation and standards. The Standard Minimum Rules for the Treatment of Prisoners, adopted in 1955 was one of the first attempts to establish base requirements for the handling of offenders. Other contributions include the U.N. World Crime Survey, the U.N. Code of Conduct for Law Enforcement Officials, and the Crime Prevention and Criminal Justice Program.

Finally, the role of the International Police Association (**INTERPOL**) is outlined. INTERPOL acts primarily as a clearinghouse for information on offenses and suspects who are believed to operate across national boundaries.

KEY TERMS

Ethnocentrism: The phenomena of culture-centeredness, by which one uses one's own culture as a benchmark against which to judge all other patterns of behavior.

Comparative Criminologist: One who studies crime and criminal justice on a cross-national level.

Procuratorate: A term used in many countries to refer to agencies with powers and responsibilities similar to those of prosecutor's offices in the United States.

Mediation Committees: Chinese civilian dispute resolution groups found throughout the country. Mediation committees successfully divert many minor offenders from handling by more formal mechanisms of justice.

Islamic Law: A system of laws, operative in some Arab countries, which is based upon the Muslim religion and especially the holy book of Islam, the Koran.

Hudud Crimes: Serious violations of Islamic law regarded as offenses against God.

> Examples: theft, adultery, sodomy, drinking alcohol, and robbery

Tazirat Crimes: Minor violations of Islamic law that are regarded as offenses against society and against individuals, not against God.

> Examples: murder, manslaughter, assault, and maiming

INTERPOL: An acronym for the International Police Association.

World Crime Surveys: Sponsored by the United Nations to provide a global portrait of criminal activity.

> Example: World Crime Surveys indicate that crimes against property are more characteristic of developed nations, while crimes against the person occur much more frequently in developing countries.

Crown Court: Established in 1971 to hear cases involving major offenses, Crown courts are headed by justices appointed by the king or queen. Twelve-member juries decide guilt or innocence, and conviction requires only a majority consensus, not unanimous agreement among jurors.

Parliament: Legislative body in England consisting of two bodies (the House of Lords and the House of Commons), established by the English Bill of Rights in 1688. Parliament has statutory authority over that of the Sovereign, and acts of Parliament are the law of the land and cannot be overruled by any court.

Act of Settlement: Passed in 1700 to reinforce the powers of Parliament and make clear the authority of judges and other officials.

Standard Minimum Rules for the Treatment of Prisoners: A set of recommendations of the United Nations adopted in 1955 at the first U.N. Congress on the Prevention of Crime and the Treatment of Offenders. The Rules call for the fair treatment of prisoners and set specific standards for housing, nutrition, exercise, and medical care.

New Scotland Yard: Headquarters for the Metropolitan Police District, which is responsible for law enforcement in London and the surrounding counties.

Criminal Justice and Public Order Act of 1994 (CJA): A return to a get-tough English anti-crime policy. The CJA selectively criminalized what had previously been especially serious violations of the civil law, made it easier to catch and convict criminals, made it harder for repeat offenders to get bail, and restricted, at least to some degree, the rights of criminal defendants.

PRACTICE TEST QUESTIONS

MULTIPLE CHOICE

16-1. Asahara, the purported leader of the Supreme Truth Sect, is accused of causing the release of deadly nerve gas in the country of _____.
   a. Taiwan
   b. Japan
   c. China
   d. Singapore

16-2. Using one's own culture as a benchmark against which to judge all other behavior patterns is called
  a. ethnocentrism.
  b. eurocentrism.
  c. hypersensitivity.
  d. fatalism.

16-3. All of the following are problems in the utilization of crime data from other countries except:
  a. differences in the definition of crime.
  b. diverse crime reporting practices.
  c. lack of crime to report.
  d. political and other influences on the reporting of crime.

16-4. The Chinese leader who resisted the use of bureaucratic agencies and relied heavily upon informal social controls was
  a. Deng Zaoping.
  b. Mao Zedong.
  c. Hwa Zsunow.
  d. Wan Kenobe.

16-5. Most minor infractions of Chinese law are dealt with through the use of
  a. arrests.
  b. military intervention.
  c. mediation committees.
  d. stern warnings from a judge.

16-6. Some human rights organizations claim that prisoners who are executed in _____ routinely serve as involuntary organ donors, and that foreigners visiting the country arrange to purchase the organs of dead prisoners for planned transplant operations.
  a. Iraq
  b. Iran
  c. China
  d. Wales

16-7. All of the following are considered *Hudud* crimes under Islamic law except:
  a. adultery.
  b. drinking alcohol.
  c. theft.
  d. murder.

16-8. Which of the following is not considered a cornerstone of British government?
  a. The Magna Carta
  b. The Bill of Rights
  c. The Declaration of Independence
  d. The Act of Settlement

16-9. Which of the following countries has the lowest rate of incarceration?
  a. Russia
  b. United States
  c. Spain
  d. Japan

16-10. The name of the police agency being created by the 15 European member nations that will facilitate the sharing of crime information between European countries and INTERPOL is
  a. Europol.
  b. Outerpol.
  c. Francopol.
  d. Commonpol.

TRUE–FALSE

_____ 16-11. China has a very bad problem with automobile theft since cars are so rare there.

_____ 16-12. Some Communist countries report only robberies and thefts which involve the property of citizens, since crimes against state-owned property fall into a separate category.

_____ 16-13. Once you have been arrested for a crime in China, your chances of acquittal by the Chinese criminal courts are virtually nonexistent.

_____ 16-14. For all its apparent harshness, the Chinese justice system is based upon a strong cultural belief in personal reformation.

_____ 16-15. Prison sentences in China do not allow for any possibility of parole.

_____ 16-16. After an execution in China, the offender's family is routinely ordered to pay for the cost of the bullet used to kill the offender.

_____ 16-17. In Iran (under Islamic law), a man was recently sentenced to be executed for bank fraud.

_____ 16-18. The 1994 passage of the Criminal Justice and Public Order Act in Great Britain marked a return to a more conciliatory, rehabilitative form of criminal justice.

_____ 16-19. Three kinds of prison exist in England: short term, medium term, and long term.

_____ 16-20. English law makes a distinction between "arrestable" and "nonarrestable" offenses, rather than felonies and misdemeanors.

_____ 16-21. Even though British police were traditionally armed only with a nightstick, recent events have caused police administrators to order all beat officers to carry a handgun at all times.

MATCHING

a. ethnocentrism
b. comparative criminologist
c. procuratorate
d. mediation committees
e. Islamic law
f. *Hudud* crimes
g. *Tazirat* crimes

h. INTERPOL
i. World Crime Surveys
j. Crown Court
k. Parliament
l. Act of Settlement
m. New Scotland Yard
n. Criminal Justice and Public Order Act 1994

_____ 16-22. using one's own culture as a benchmark against which to judge all other patterns of behavior.

_____ 16-23. A set of recommendations of the United Nations adopted in 1955 at the first U.N. Congress on the Prevention of Crime and the Treatment of Offenders.

_____ 16-24. A person who studies crime and criminal justice on a cross-national level.

_____ 16-25. Legislative body in England consisting of the House of Lords and the House of Commons.

_____ 16-26. A term used in many countries to refer to agencies with powers and responsibilities similar to those of prosecutor's offices in the United States.

_____ 16-27. Sponsored by the United Nations to provide a global portrait of criminal activity.

_____ 16-28. Chinese civilian dispute resolution groups designed to divert minor offenders from handling by more formal mechanisms of justice.

_____ 16-29. Headquarters for the London Metropolitan Police District.

_____ 16-30. Minor violations of Islamic law that are regarded as offenses against society and against individuals, not against God.

_____ 16-31. Passed in 1700 to reinforce the powers of Parliament and make clear the authority of judges and other officials.

DISCUSSION EXERCISES

1. Students reading this text typically view the types of offenses taken seriously and lightly in other countries with some amusement. For example, Islamic law calls for 100 lashes for fornication and flogging and stoning to death for adultery. However, manslaughter and assault are almost considered to be the equivalent of our civil offenses. Can you think of any deviant behaviors that we in the United States strictly prohibit or implicitly condone that other cultures might find odd?

2. Should some attempt be made to create a more universal code of criminal behavior? Are there any types of criminal behavior that might be globally forbidden?

3. Why do you think international incarceration rates (like those expressed in Figure 16-2) vary so much? Do you see any common characteristics between countries that rely heavily on incarceration?

17

THE FUTURE OF CRIMINAL JUSTICE

CHAPTER SUMMARY

The chapter begins with the story of Kirk Bloodsworth, who was vindicated and released after serving nine years in prison for a crime he did not commit. The use of DNA testing cleared him of any wrongdoing, and it is clear that the technological advances of the coming years will continue to have a greater impact on the criminal justice system. Criminalistics, or the use of technology in the service of criminal investigation, has always played an important role in establishing the guilt or innocence of suspects. A variety of identification methods, including the Bertillon system of measuring the characteristics of certain body parts, and the use of fingerprinting are outlined.

Some of the emerging technologies in criminalistics, including DNA Profiling, On-Line Clearinghouses for criminal justice information, Computer-aided investigations and computer-based training are examined. Some of the problems in the implementation of these new technologies is discussed, including the reluctance or inability of local police departments to utilize the new techniques and the misuse of emerging technologies by both law enforcement and criminals.

Cybercrime is examined next and is classified as the new white-collar crime. A brief examination of traditional forms of white-collar crime is made, including such crimes as fraud, embezzlement, and money laundering. The area of occupational crime is discussed along with the importance of access to criminal activity. The computer and sophisticated knowledge of its use is essential to the accomplishment of high technology crime, and the chapter outlines some of the new terminology associated with this new type of criminal endeavor. The prosecution of computer and high-tech crime is becoming an increasingly complicated and serious undertaking, and the variety of types of computer crime is also increasing. Unauthorized access to data, willful destruction of data, and data manipulation are three of the general areas of computer crime that are discussed in detail. Combating computer crime is a tough process since the perpetrators tend to be young, very well-educated, and the crimes are difficult to detect.

Terrorism is another area that will become of increasing concern to Americans in the future. Although the number of total deaths caused by terrorist acts has not been increasing dramatically, the number of individual incidents have continued to rise, as have the number of fringe groups who have resorted to terrorist methods to achieve their political ends. The rules of terrorism developed by Gwynn Nettler are discussed, as are methods that are currently being implemented to control terrorism in the future.

The chapter concludes with an examination of the role that technology will likely play in the limiting or expansion of individual rights. The Second, Fourth, Fifth, Sixth, Eighth, and Fourteenth Amendments to the U.S. Constitution are examined in light of ever-changing technology and its impact on the rights of individual citizens.

KEY TERMS

Forensic Anthropology: The application of anthropological principles and techniques in the service of criminal investigation.

DNA Profiling: The use of biological residue found at the scene of a crime for genetic comparisons in aiding the identification of criminal suspects.

Expert Systems: Computer hardware and software which attempt to duplicate the decision-making processes used by skilled investigators in the analysis of evidence and in the recognition of patterns which such evidence might represent.

High-technology Crime: Violations of the criminal law whose commission depends upon, makes use of, and often targets sophisticated and advanced technology.

Computer Crime: Any crime which takes advantage of computer-based technology in its commission. This definition highlights the manner in which a crime is committed, more than it does the target of the offense.

White-collar Crime: Nonviolent crime for financial gain committed by means of deception by persons having professional status or specialized technical skills during the everyday pursuit of their business endeavors.

Occupational Crime: Any act punishable by law which is committed through opportunity created in the course of an occupation that is legal.

Corporate Crime: A violation of a criminal statute by a corporate entity or by its executives, employees, or agents acting on behalf of and for the benefit of the corporation, partnership, or other form of business entity.

Computer Hacker: Computer hobbyists or professionals, generally with advanced programming skills. Today the term "hacker" has taken on a sinister connotation, and includes those hobbyists who are bent on illegally accessing the computers of others or who attempt to demonstrate their technological prowess through computerized acts of vandalism.

Federal Interest Computers: Those which (1) are the property of the federal government, (2) belong to financial institutions, or (3) are located in a state other than the one in which the criminal perpetrator is operating. Federal Interest Computers are defined by the Computer Fraud and Abuse Act, as amended in 1986.

Data Encryption: Methods used to encode computerized information.

Computer Virus: A small computer program which is designed to secretly invade systems and modify either the way in which they operate or alter the information they store. Viruses are destructive software which may effectively vandalize computers of all sizes.

> Example: The Michaelangelo virus was created by a computer hacker to crash the hard disk of infected computers when the internal clock of the computer reached a specified day.

Terrorism: A violent act or an act dangerous to human life in violation of the criminal laws of the United States or of any state to intimidate or coerce a government, the civilian population, or any segment thereof, in furtherance of political or social objectives.

Cybercrime: Crime committed with the use of computers; another term for computer crime.

Criminalistics: The use of technology in the service of criminal investigation; the application of scientific techniques to the detection and evaluation of criminal evidence.

Criminalist: The term applied to police crime scene analysts and laboratory personnel versed in criminalistics.

KEY CASES

Holt v. *Sarver*: (1970) The federal district court for the Eastern District of Arkansas defined cruel and unusual punishment to be that which is "shocking to the conscience of reasonably civilized people."

Daubert v. *Merrell Dow Pharmaceuticals, Inc.*: (1993) The results of DNA testing can be acceptable in criminal trials as long as the techniques employed meet the test for admission of scientific evidence published under the Federal Rules of Evidence.

PRACTICE TEST QUESTIONS

MULTIPLE CHOICE

17-1. The _____, formerly known as the Technology Assessment Program Information Center (TAPIC), performs yearly assessments of key technological needs and opportunities facing the justice system.
  a. Law Enforcement Assistance Administration (LEAA)
  b. National Law Enforcement Technology Center (NLETC)
  c. Office of Law Enforcement Organization (OLEO)
  d. International Technology Protection Program (ITPP)

17-2. The case of *Daubert* v. *Merrell Dow Pharmaceuticals* proved to be important in the acceptance of _____ in criminal trials.
  a. fingerprints
  b. serial killer profiles
  c. DNA profiles
  d. computer-enhanced images

17-3. All of the following are considered ways of controlling access to data except:
  a. physical security.
  b. passwords.
  c. data encryption.
  d. all of the above

17-4. Students who access university administrative records in order to change grades would be committing
  a. willful destruction of data.
  b. data manipulation.
  c. data encryption.
  d. data diddling.

17-5. If a computer is the property of the federal government or belongs to a financial institution, or is located in a state other than the one in which the criminal perpetrator is operating, it is classified as a
    a. federal interest computer.
    b. interstate compact computer.
    c. federated computer.
    d. institutionalized computer.

17-6. In 1995 Sheik Oma Abdel-Rahmam and other Muslim fundamentalists were convicted of the terrorist bombing of the _____ in New York City.
    a. Statute of Liberty
    b. World Trade Center
    c. United Nations Building
    d. Rockefeller Center

17-7. All of the following are part of Gwynn Nettler's Rules of Terrorism except:
    a. no rules.
    b. no innocents.
    c. no prisoners.
    d. no clarity.

17-8. A drug used in the treatment of alcoholics which causes a violent reaction when alcohol is ingested is
    a. Depro-Provera.
    b. Antabuse.
    c. Tylenol.
    d. Pharmacol.

17-9. As society becomes more dependent upon computers, the damage potential of viruses will likely _____.
    a. increase
    b. decrease
    c. stay the same
    d. we have no way of knowing

17-10. The Amendment which is most concerned with the equal protection of the laws is the
    a. Fourth.
    b. Fifth.
    c. Eighth.
    d. Fourteenth.

TRUE–FALSE

_____ 17-11. Fingerprinting, which became widespread as a crime-fighting technique in the late 1800s, provided one of the first nearly foolproof methods of identification available to investigators.

_____ 17-12. Modern criminalistics depends heavily on ballistics, which involves the reconstruction of the likeness of a decomposed or dismembered body.

_____ 17-13. One of the most prevalent problems in computer crime is the unauthorized duplication of copyrighted software.

_____ 17-14. Logic bombs, worms, and Trojan horse routines are all forms of computer viruses.

_____ 17-15. The total cost to American taxpayers of the white-collar crime generated through the savings and loan failures of the 1980s and early 1990s have been estimated to be as high as $500 billion dollars over the next thirty years—more money than has been lost in all bank robberies throughout the course of American history.

_____ 17-16. It appears that incidents of terrorism perpetrated by foreign agents against the United States are starting to decline, and most experts agree that technological advances will cause an almost total disappearance of terrorism within the next 20 years.

_____ 17-17. The Brady Law, named after James Brady, who was shot in the head by John Hinckley, requires a thirty-day waiting period before any gun can be purchased, as well as a thorough background check by the FBI of anyone wishing to purchase any gun.

_____ 17-18. The U.S. Supreme Court has held that such modern technological procedures as blood-alcohol tests, and the involuntary gathering of blood, hair, semen, or tissue samples are all acceptable so long as the procedures used in gathering the self-incriminating evidence do not "shock the conscience."

_____ 17-19. The U.S. Supreme Court has held that so-called "chemical castration" through the use of drugs such as Depo-Provera do not violate the Eighth Amendment prohibition against cruel and unusual punishment, so long as the offender has a choice between prison and the drug treatment.

_____ 17-20. Until the introduction of the American National Standard for Information Systems—Fingerprint Identification—Data Format for Information Interchange in 1986, the comparison of fingerprint data between different law enforcement agencies was difficult or impossible.

MATCHING

a. forensic anthropology
b. DNA Profiling
c. expert systems
d. criminalistics
e. terrorism
f. white-collar crime
g. cybercrime
h. computer virus
i. computer hacker
j. data encryption

_____ 17-21. Another term for computer crime or crime involving the use of computers.

_____ 17-22. The application of anthropological principles and techniques to a criminal investigation.

_____ 17-23. The use of a blood sample or other residue found at the scene of a crime for genetic comparisons in aiding the identification of criminal suspects.

_____ 17-24. Computer software which attempts to replicate the decision-making processes used by skilled investigators in the analysis of evidence.

_____ 17-25. Crime for financial gain, committed by means of deception by someone who has specialized technical skills, during the everyday pursuit of their business endeavors.

_____ 17-26. A computer hobbyist who illegally accesses the computers of others to demonstrate technological superiority.

_____ 17-27. Used to encode computerized information as a method of thwarting cybercriminals.

_____ 17-28. Destructive computer software designed to vandalize computers of all sizes.

_____ 17-29. A violent act or an act dangerous to human life designed to intimidate or coerce a government in furtherance of political or social objectives.

_____ 17-30. The application of scientific techniques to the detection and evaluation of criminal evidence.

DISCUSSION EXERCISES

1. How much privacy are you willing to give up in the fight against crime? Would you be willing to be under constant video surveillance if it meant a 40 - 50% reduction in violent crime? What assurances do we have that offenders won't simply ignore these high-tech devices and commit the crime anyway?

    Is there such a thing as having too much centralized information available on an individual? Take a look at your social security card—it clearly states that your social security number is not to be used for identification purposes. Yet some stores routinely refuse to let customers write checks for purchases unless the customer provides his or her social security number on the check. How do you explain this paradox?

2. Throughout our history, police have claimed that if they were just given the proper tools, they could really do something about the crime problem. For example, law enforcement officials at the turn of the century argued that as soon as the police force became "motorized" with the newfangled automobile, they would be able to apprehend offenders with ease. The same claim was made for mobile radios, machine guns, mobile data terminals, cellular phones, and so forth. In some cities, the cost of equipping a police car with all of the electronic equipment and special features police claim as essential to their effectiveness approaches the actual cost of the car itself! Do you think technology will ever be able to give police departments the edge they have been looking for in the fight against crime? Will the reactive nature of policing mean that cops will always be at least one step behind the offenders, or will police eventually get ahead of the offenders in the fight against crime?

3. With the increased reliance on DNA testing, surveillance equipment, and other tools, is it possible that the guilt of the defendant will be so clear-cut that there will be no need for a jury trial? Will there be a role in the next century for jurors who have little technological sophistication? Will attorneys be able to utilize "technologically inept" as an acceptable challenge for cause/peremptory challenge?

SURVEILLANCE ZOOMING IN WITH HIGH-TECH
But Critics Fear for Privacy

Byline: John Larrabee

Someday soon, travelers landing at a major airport could be made to pass their hands under an electronic sensor that detects small particles of heroin and cocaine.

A crack addict convicted of burglary could be sentenced to wear an electronic bracelet that alerts probation officers if drugs are detected in his sweat.

And a tanker truck cruising toward a border checkpoint could be scanned by a camera that snaps X-ray-type pictures of the cargo before the driver even slows down.

Such high-tech surveillance could become commonplace by the end of the century.

The development worries privacy advocates, who fear that the war on drug users and dealers is driving the government into increasingly sophisticated snooping on citizens. Drug agents say the technology is necessary to keep up with modern smugglers.

A five-year effort by the federal Counterdrug Technology Assessment Center will help put a new generation of sleuthing gear into the hands of law enforcement, from sonar devices that inspect sealed drums to drug-test kits that can be carried in squad cars.

White House drug czar Lee Brown says the technology is needed and is nothing to worry about: "I don't see how there's even an issue with civil liberties here. Its about our kids. We're using new technology to deal with those who are exporting poison to our children."

Others aren't so thrilled.

"The priority is more on monitoring the law-abiding population than keeping track of the people the police already know are dealing drugs," says Robert Ellis Smith, editor of the Privacy Journal. "It's a vision of America that's quite different from mine."

To many, one of the hottest new gizmos is also one of the most troubling. Using new computer technology, the "facial recognition system" lets police photograph crowds and check digitized faces against a database of criminal suspects.

Immigration officers in El Paso already use a new surveillance camera to photograph suspects and identify them by name if their face is in a database of 10,000 people. The system supposedly also can identify people who have aged or are wearing disguises.

This system could be used to identify suspicious travelers as they disembark from planes or to scan rock concert crowds to see if any faces match a database of drug dealers.

But defense lawyers question whether the equipment will live up to the hype and whether matching a digitized face to a person in a crowd is "probable cause" for police to search or arrest someone.

"We're a nation of Forrest Gumps for letting them get away with this," says John Henry Hingson III, former president of the National Association of Criminal Defense Lawyers.

But Arvid Larson, a consultant to the drug czar, expects police to win court challenges. "The new technology usually prevails, but sometimes it takes years. DNA evidence is still challenged, and we went through 30 or 40 years of fingerprint issues."

Hingson, an Oregon City, Ore., defense lawyer, says the equipment is a threat to civil liberties. "The real casualty of the war on drugs could be the privacy rights of law-abiding Americans. What they're doing by unveiling these stealthy, smart weapons is instill in people a fear and suspicion of the government, and that's really stupid."

But to Brown, who steps down as drug czar in January, the technology will make police more respectful of civil liberties, not less, because it's "less intrusive. Surveillance technology that can isolate a criminal's voice in a crowded, noisy room protects the rights of others."

Private business also is interested in this technology.

"If these (cameras) go up in malls or retail stores, they could collect data on people for marketing purposes," says David Banisar of the Electronic Privacy Information Center. "They'll know you've been in the store and what you bought, and they'll use that to determine what sort of advertising to hit you with."

Reprinted with permission of *USA Today*

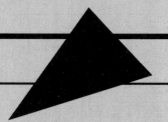

EMPLOYMENT OPPORTUNITIES IN THE CRIMINAL JUSTICE FIELD

CRIMINAL JUSTICE CAREERS

Most students pursuing degrees in higher education will one day seek employment. The criminal justice area (including private security) is one of the most attractive career fields available to today's students. It is an area in which opportunities abound and where career choices continue to grow. Graduates of both 2-year and 4-year colleges and universities can typically choose from among careers in law enforcement, courts, corrections, and the law (although a law degree is required for the practice of law). Opportunities include careers with (1) law enforcement agencies, whether as a uniformed officer, laboratory technician, crime scene investigator, photographer, or fingerprint or communications expert; (2) probation and parole offices; (3) juvenile justice agencies; (4) prisons and jails; (5) the courts; (6) law firms; (7) private security companies; and (8) industries needing private investigative services.

Many local criminal justice and private security agencies advertise under the "employment" section of local newspapers, while federal agencies announce vacancies through the Office of Personnel Management's job listings. Recruiters from a variety of agencies often visit college campuses around graduation time, and telephone calls to such agencies can uncover employment opportunities not otherwise announced. Addresses and phone numbers for many federal criminal justice agencies are listed in the "Careers Boxes" found throughout your textbook, *Criminal Justice Today.*

APPLYING FOR A JOB

Once potential employers have been identified, interested job applicants should submit application packets to the addresses specified by the employers. An application packet generally consists of (1) a cover letter expressing the applicant's interest in the position, (2) a completed resume (also called a vitae), and (3) a list of references (often listed on the resume) that the potential employer can contact. Applicants may also be asked to submit an agency-specific official application form, college and university transcripts, completed reference letters, and an essay describing their career goals. Applicants for federal employment must usually include a completed SF-171 ("Standard Form 171: Application for Federal Employment"), or the Optional Application for Federal Employment: form OF 612.

Employers will typically select a number of promising individuals from among the pool of applicants for additional screening. The second step in employment screening may consist of an interview and a battery of job-specific tests, such as a psychological inventories, physical agility tests, and written examinations to insure that candidates are qualified for available positions. Drug testing (urinalysis) and a background investigation are also part of the employment screening process of many criminal justice and private security agencies.

Employers are often not interested in receiving many items that an applicant may feel are important in an application packet. Hence, it is not necessary to submit newspaper clippings, scrapbook entries, photocopies of awards, etc. unless and until the employment process proceeds further, and the employer expresses interest in seeing such materials.

WRITING A COVER LETTER

The cover letter that accompanies a job application packet is often the first thing a potential employer sees. As is true for all other elements of the application package, a cover letter should be neatly typed or word processed. Word processed letters should be printed on high quality printers, such as laser or ink-jet printers. Dot-matrix printers should be avoided—especially those with worn ribbons. Cover letters should express interest in the position applied for, should offer a brief summary of the applicants qualifications, and should refer the reader to an accompanying resume. Cover letters must also contain the applicant's address and phone number in order to facilitate continued contact with the potential employer. A sample cover letter is included in this appendix.

WRITING A RÉSUMÉ

A sample one-page resume is also included in this section. Experienced job applicants may have more lengthy resumes. Any resume, however, should include the following sections: (1) objective or career goals, (2) education, (3) job-related experience, (4) any honors the applicant may have received, (5) relevant hobbies, (6) a list of references available for contact by the employer.

Resumes should be neatly typed or word processed and printed on good quality paper. Some applicants have prepared disk- or software-based resumes, often with multimedia features which can be run on employer's computers. Others now list their qualifications on the Internet and on the World Wide Web. While you may have the ability to create such "high-tech" applications, remember that most employers have neither the technological know-how nor the time needed to review such materials. Hence, in most situations, traditional printed resumes are still a necessity.

THE IMPORTANCE OF REFERENCES

Anyone listed as a reference on your resume should be informed that you will be using their name in conjunction with a job search. Hence, should a potential employer contact them, they will not be surprised. Likewise, anyone who objects to being listed should immediately be removed from your list of references. Whenever possible, it is a good idea to ask potential references how they feel about serving as references for you. You should only select individuals who you feel confident will provide the best references.

THE EMPLOYMENT INTERVIEW

If your application makes it through an initial screening, you will be invited for an interview. Applicants invited for a job interview should follow two important rules: (1) be punctual, and (2) dress appropriately.

Most interviewers will make some effort to put job candidates at ease. The interview will probably begin with a handshake and a smile, and the interviewer may make some introductory comments about the agency and job expectations associated with the position applied for.

During the interview process it is generally a good strategy to stay away from personal questions or intimate observations. Similarly, avoid initiating discussions centered on politics, religion, and most personal preferences. Most interviewers know that personal questions that are too prying are inappropriate, although job-related personal questions may be raised. So, for example, law enforcement employers may question applicants about their personal experience with controlled substances, or about crimes or misdemeanors in the person's background. The applicant who refuses to answer such questions will probably not be hired.

The job interview is your opportunity to sell yourself. Although you won't want to sound as though you are "bragging," an employer will expect you to describe your experiences and personal qualities that make hiring you a good decision.

PERSONAL APPEARANCE AND THE INTERVIEW PROCESS

While styles of dress have changed significantly during the last decade or two, most employers still expect job applicants to have a neat and well-groomed appearance. Remember, once hired, the job applicant takes on a new role: that of agency representative. Ask yourself what kind of a public image you will be expected to project as an official representative of the agency with which you are interviewing, and dress accordingly. Men may conclude that a suit and tie, or sports coat with dress slacks is appropriate attire for an interview, while women may want to dress conservatively—and include dress shoes (not necessarily heels) in the outfit they select. Overly casual clothes are to be avoided in most employment interview settings.

SALARY AND OTHER EXPECTATIONS

Students entering the criminal justice career field with a 2-year associate of arts degree, or a 4-year bachelor of arts degree, can expect to earn about $18,000–$32,000 during their first year of work. Salaries vary by agency and geographic location. Criminal justice agencies located in urban areas generally pay higher salaries because the cost of living is higher in cities than it is in rural locales. Similarly, federal agencies typically pay higher salaries than state and local agencies, although cities and states with a healthy tax base are often able to offer competitive wages to well-qualified candidates.

Salary should not be the job candidate's only consideration. Other benefits, including retirement programs, paid vacations, sick leave policies, employer-provided health coverage, employer-paid life insurance, survivor's benefits, uniform allowance (if applicable), and the quality of the work environment should all be considered. Quality of the work environment can be measured in terms of working hours expected of new employees, available shift hours (if any), routine types of assignment, commradere among fellow employees, and attitudes of supervisors.

While benefits such as life insurance and retirement may not seem significant to many first-time job applicants, their significance is often later realized—especially as lifestyle changes such as marriage, parenthood, and the natural effects of aging make themselves felt.

A sample cover letter and sample resume appear on the two pages that follow.

Drug Enforcement Administration
Office of Personnel, Recruitment, and Placement
600-700 Army-Navy Drive
Arlington, VA 22202   September 28, 19XX

Dear Sir/Madam:

I am applying for the position of special agent, as announced recently in the Office of Personnel Management's job listings.

I hold an Associate of Arts degree in criminal justice from Southridge Community College in Southridge, New York, and will be receiving a Bachelor of Arts degree in criminal justice in May of 1997 from Southridge State University.

My résumé, along with a completed SF-171 "Application for Federal Employment" form, is enclosed for your use. References are included on the resume, as well as listed on the form.

I look forward to hearing from you.

Thank you.

Sincerely,

Jane A. Student
5 Legacy Court
Any Town, NY 11222
Phone: 212-555-1234

5 Legacy Court
Any Town, NY 11222
Phone: 212-555-1234

Jane A. Student

OBJECTIVE   To work in the criminal justice system—preferably as a law enforcement officer.

EDUCATION   September 1995–May 1997   Southridge State U.   Southridge, NY
• Bachelor of Arts in Criminal Justice, 1997

September 1993–May 1995   Southridge Community College
• Associate of Arts in Criminal Justice, 1995

EXPERIENCE   January 1997–May 1997
• Law Enforcement Intern, Southridge County Sheriff's Dept., Southridge, NY
• Part-Time Security Guard, Security Services, Inc., The Mall, Southridge, NY
• D.A.R.E student volunteer, Southridge High School, 1993

HONORS   • Graduated Summa Cum Laude, Southridge State University
• President, Gamma Gamma Mu Sorority
• Criminal Justice Student of the Year, 1996

HOBBIES   • Computer Programming
• Internet Browsing
• Amateur Radio: Novice License, 1993; General Class, 1994.
• Collecting Police Department Shoulder Patches

REFERENCES

Prof. John Justice	Prof. Susan Scales	Prof. Ima Lot
333 Stark Bldg.	335 Stark Bldg.	101 Old Main
Southridge State University	Southridge State University	Southridge C.C. College
Southridge, NY 11223	Southridge, NY 11223	Southridge, NY 11224

Transcripts and the names and addresses of additional references are available upon request.